OUTDOOR TRAINING

For employee effectiveness

Mark Tuson

INSTITUTE OF PERSONNEL MANAGEMENT

First published in 1994

Phototypeset in Times by
The Comp-Room, Aylesbury
and printed in Great Britain by
Short Run Press, Exeter

British Library Cataloguing in Publication Data

Tuson, Mark
    Outdoor Training for Employee
    Effectiveness. – (Developing Skills
    Series)
    I. Title   II. Series
    658.3124

    ISBN 0-85292-549-2

The views expressed in this book are the author's own and
may not necessarily reflect those of the IPM.

INSTITUTE OF PERSONNEL MANAGEMENT
IPM House, Camp Road, Wimbledon, London SW19 4UX
Tel: 081-946-9100   Fax: 081-947-2570
Registered office as above. Registered Charity No. 215797
A company limited by guarantee. Registered in England No. 198002

Contents

Acknowledgements		vii
Introduction		viii

1 What is Outdoor Training — 1
Origins and influences — 1
The learning cycle — 6
Different types of programme — 7
Safety considerations — 8

2 What Can the Outdoors Offer My Organisation? — 10
Why it is so useful — 10
The skills and issues addressed — 13

3 Defining the Objectives — 18
Training needs analysis — 18
The design process — 23

4 Structuring a Programme — 29
Basic assumptions — 29
The learning process — 34
Safety net (physical) — 38
Safety net (emotional) — 46

5 Task Design — 60
Simulation — 60
Impact — 68
Safety — 71
Examples of outdoor tasks and projects — 74

6 Review Design — 93
Analysis of a task review — 94
Examples of review designs — 98

7 Transfer — 115
The basis for transfer and implementation — 115
Putting it into practice — 118

8 Evaluation   125

9 Resourcing an Outdoor Programme   128
    The training staff   128
    The outdoor staff   135
    The venue   140

10 Putting It All Together   143
    The programme   143
    Trainer's notes   147
    Activities, with review guidelines   148

Appendix: Some useful models for review   165

Acknowledgements

A great number of people and organisations have wittingly or unwittingly contributed or inspired the ideas and concepts that make up the bulk of this book.

In terms of a 'house' of knowledge, the concepts making up the foundations and a large part of the external walls were provided by Harvey Peters and his organisation Minerva Training; many of the ideas and much of the experience forming the other walls were made possible or contributed by John Charlish. The internal partitions, the divisions between different levels and the doors that connect the different areas are my responsibility.

A great many other people have contributed to this house, and I am extremely grateful to them. They include: John Campbell, Dave Savage, Peter Mason, John Walsh, and many more.

One individual who deserves specific recognition is Paul Haves, whose support and trust whilst I have been gaining the knowledge and experience that goes into this book, has been constant and unflagging.

As yet the house does not have a roof: it is still growing, and I hope it will keep on doing so; the day the roof goes on will be the day I start looking for a new line of work.

Introduction

On top of a cliff face in the Peak District in Derbyshire, a man in his late twenties is standing ready to abseil down; he is very scared and only there because he feels he will be letting the rest of his team down if he does not do it. They have already done it, enjoyed it immensely and are waiting at the bottom for him. The instructor on the top with him looks faintly bored, and she tells him to get on with it – everyone is waiting for him, the group will soon run out of time and fail the task, and it will be *his* fault. After hesitating for a while he starts to move over the edge, panics, says he cannot do it and comes scrambling back to the top in tears, which are then exacerbated by the shouts from below wanting to know what is going on, and why the delay. It is likely that he took little or no part in the subsequent review of the task and became very negative about the whole programme, its objectives and possibly the organisation that sent him on it.

In a cave just South of the Brecon Beacons in South Wales, a group of six have just stopped, and the instructor has checked that everyone is still OK (later on, this function will be carried out by the group and the instructor will merely monitor it). They then explore a number of route options (using the instructor as a technical resource) and select the one they feel is most appropriate. Halfway along the passage one of the group members becomes unhappy and feels that he cannot go any further. He says so and the group stop, re-evaluate their options and find an alternative, more acceptable route; they then compensate for the loss of time by modifying their overall plan, and if necessary reducing their overall objective. Later, part of the task review focused on allowing for contingencies when planning and setting objectives, and similar situations that had occurred in the workplace.

The two scenarios described above are drawn from observation of management training programmes using the outdoors. The first illustrates graphically how the outdoors can be misused and the potential effects of this misuse. The second illustrates how it can also be used in a very positive, relevant and non-threatening manner.

This book is all about how to avoid the first scenario and achieve the second. It is the result of six years' personal experience delivering commercial programmes in this field, and eighteen years' accumulated experience of the organisation where I learned how to do it.

For a long time, the use of the outdoors as a training medium was perceived by the majority of organisations as too complex, unconventional and specialised for their own 'normal' trainers to get involved in. Today, more and more client trainers are becoming involved in designing and running their own outdoor programmes. It is to encourage this process that I have chosen to write this book. Its aims are simple:

> to encourage the active involvement of clients and their trainers in the process of designing and running their own outdoor programmes

> to describe a system or framework for designing and running programmes, so that client trainers can slot themselves into an appropriate role and direct the providers filling the other roles

> to promote the use of the outdoors as a means of developing individuals, teams and organisations.

In order to achieve this, I have structured it so that readers can use it to help them:

> familiarise themselves with the potential of outdoor training and the issues involved in its use

> maximise the benefit and relevance of outdoor programmes commissioned from providers

> get involved in the design and planning of such programmes

> get involved in the delivery of such programmes

> design, deliver and resource their own programmes.

There is no attempt to minimise the inherent difficulties: designing and running an outdoor programme involves specific skills and raises issues that many trainers are not familiar with. For example, most trainers are aware of the facilitative style that is fundamental to most outdoor programmes. However, to be really effective requires a significant amount of practice on outdoor programmes, helping the participants to deal with (and process in a useful manner) the vast amount of information, considerable emotions or passions, and real work-related issues generated by the medium. The ability to generate these is, of course, one of the strengths of this type of training.

The physical and emotional welfare of the participants is a major area that requires careful and well-thought-out handling. This has always been a major issue and has been highlighted by the media on a number of recent occasions. *The applicability and transferability* of learning from such programmes to the workplace is another issue that often needs to be addressed in promoting it to an organisation. *Evaluation* of the effect of such programmes has also traditionally been perceived as difficult, which can sometimes make it difficult for trainers to justify them.

None of these issues, however, is insurmountable, and they are counterbalanced by the much wider range of advantages that are a consequence of greater involvement by the client organisation.

The first part of the book discusses the origins of outdoor training, and the basic assumptions or operating principles that I feel underlie its ethical use as a commercial training medium. It is imperative that anyone involved in outdoor programmes has thought through the issues involved, and their own views or values, before being challenged on the edge of a cliff or halfway through a review to justify their actions and method of operating, either to the participants or to the client. I have described my own views on these matters, which can either be adopted as they stand, developed further or used as a prompt list to develop your own principles.

In the next part of the book I have taken a particular method that I use for designing and running outdoor programmes, and described it by splitting it into a number of interlocking systems. Each relates to a different area or issue, and is described in a different section or chapter of the book. These divisions are perhaps slightly artificial – in reality they form a single complex system – and I have adopted this approach purely for ease of presentation and comprehension.

The particular system described combines very clear defined objectives with review sessions in which the trainer's main role is to guide and, if necessary, structure the communication process. This is so that the participants are able to present their experiences without being influenced by the other group members (or the trainer), so that there is a real and genuine basis from which the group can draw conclusions and make adaptations. On occasion the trainer might intervene with some direct feedback if ·an issue is being glossed over – or perhaps to refocus the group on their objectives.

The result is a programme that is genuinely experiential, positive and enjoyable, and in which the trainer can build an open and ongoing relationship with the group. It is particularly effective when it comes to transferring the results back to the workplace, because it emphasises throughout the participants' ownership of the outcomes and results of the tasks and reviews, and hence the overall programme's objectives. Although there are other ways of running outdoor programmes just as effectively, such ownership of the results by the participants will prove crucial to their success.

I have assumed that if you decide to design and run your own programme, then you will need to hire in a specialist outdoor organisation to manage that element of the programme, and specifically to help design the tasks and take responsibility for resourcing and running them safely. To this end I have given a set of criteria against which to assess the expertise and experience of such organisations.

This is a confused and difficult area, especially because of the lack of legislation and the proliferation of organisations purporting to provide such services. Differentiating between their respective levels of competence both indoors and outdoors can be a difficult task to carry out effectively, although of course absolutely imperative.

Finally, I have not written a text book; this is a form of training that is still growing and developing, with new concepts and ideas being added all the time. The ideas that form the basis of this book have been subject to constant review and modification over much of the last six years, and I certainly do not intend to stop that process just because I have taken time out to write them down. Much more importantly, if you choose to use this book, neither should you.

——————— 1 ———————
What Is Outdoor Training?

In any book of this sort the first area to be addressed must be what is meant by outdoor training, as it is a term that covers a broad spectrum of activity in the training and development field. It is also an emotive term since it is a subject on which people often hold strong and conflicting views. These can arise from different perceptions of what exactly is meant by the term – at one extreme it might involve 30 minutes' blindfold exercise on the front lawn of the venue, at the other a five-day cross-country skiing expedition in the mountains of Norway living in snow holes. The range of activities that might be involved in a programme is immense and could include initiative tasks, orienteering, caving, abseiling and climbing, sailing, mountaineering, gorge crossing, and complex day-long exercises that involve several of these.

The outdoor portion of a programme is only part of the issue; there is also the question of review: in different styles of programme the time spent discussing the outcomes and implications of the outdoor tasks can vary from 5 per cent of the course time to 80 per cent. There is then the style of review to look at. It may be pedagogic: 'This is how you did this task; this is how it should be done – so you need to make the following changes'; or anagogic: exploring the task outcomes with the group or individual, and then facilitating their search for ways of performing more effectively.

Finally there might well be a specific model that is being used as a basis for the programme, as programmes are often structured around a particular concept such as Adair's Action Centred Leadership, or Margerison and McCann's team management systems, or the leadership and teambuilding models in Kenneth Blanchard's *One Minute Manager* books. All these and many more can be used effectively.

Origins and influences

To understand how the term outdoor training came to cover such

1

a broad range of activities it is necessary to look at its origins.

The most obvious influence comes from Outward Bound programmes run by the Outward Bound Trust, an organisation that has been operating since 1941. One of their original objectives was to develop young merchant seamen and help give them the self-reliance and strength of character needed to survive the truly horrendous conditions they had to endure during the Second World War. These were very successful and they still run programmes aimed at developing young people's character and determination today.* I can vouch for the effectiveness of such programmes, having taken part in one as a 17-year-old in the mid-1970s.

This sort of traditional outward bound programme is very much task-centred with comparatively little or no time spent in review, although there is a strong element of coaching during the tasks from the group tutor. It is likely to last between 8 and 14 days, and the tasks themselves are demanding and graduated, often culminating in a two- or three-day solo expedition through wild country. This sort of programme is really aimed at developing individuals holistically or on a broad front, as it presents them with a series of challenging experiences carefully designed to stretch their limits mentally and emotionally without ever pushing them too far; in the model shown opposite, we are talking about individuals having the opportunity to move out of their comfort zones and stretch themselves as much as they can without crossing the border into the panic zone, an experience which is called a frontier experience. To achieve this there is inevitably some physical pressure on the participants, and one of the main roles of the tutor in this type of programme is to monitor the physical and mental state of the participants and ensure that it is kept within safe limits. Learning from this type of programme is almost entirely self-generated by the individual, and any transfer of learning to personal and work environments is also self-managed. The next influence that comes to mind is that of the various

---

* To avoid confusion I should point out that 'outward bound' is a term also used to describe one particular type of outdoor programme developed by the Outward Bound Trust; Trust programmes are not necessarily 'outward bound' in the sense described above.

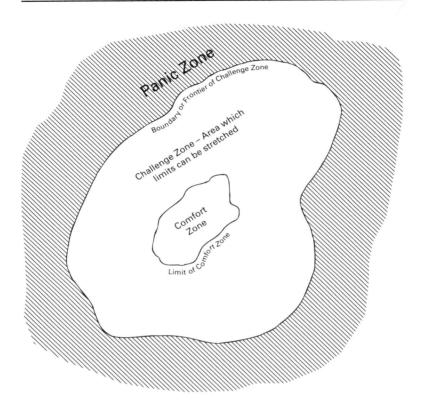

armed forces. They have contributed in three areas: firstly the concept of using outdoor or physically demanding tasks to develop teams as well as individuals; secondly the concept of using short problem-solving tasks to assess potential and actual leadership and teamworking skills; and finally the use of high ropes courses, a medium that seems once again to be growing in popularity.

The forces have always had a major commitment to developing effective teams (and leaders) and the nature of the work often makes it appropriate to do this in an outdoor environment. Since the First World War the changing nature of conflicts has necessitated a major change in the hierarchical nature of the organisation. Firstly the increasingly complex nature of the work has required a great deal of specialisation in even the smallest unit, creating small teams where there is a high level of mutual dependence. Secondly, and in parallel with this process, the level at which significant decisions are made has moved down the ladder of command. If the First World War was a generals' war, the Second was a subalterns', and the Falklands and Kuwait (not to mention Northern Ireland) were and are very definitely the corporals' domain.

With changing needs the methods changed, and towards the end of the Second World War Rowallan Company was set up to train potential officers in leadership and teamworking skills. The methods used were very similar to those used in outward bound programmes, although the focus was changed to meet the different objectives. It was again highly successful, and still exists today in a modified form, carrying out much the same function, developing leadership skills in potential officers who are not yet ready to attend Sandhurst.

Finally in the early 1950s the army started a process called Adventure Training, of which one objective was to develop leadership and teamworking skills in high-pressure situations. All young soldiers, junior NCOs, and young officers are encouraged to become involved in outdoor pursuits and then, as their skills develop, to start looking after and leading others on expeditions and trips. These are often very adventurous and create the situations in which the skills can be practised for real.*

The second area of contribution is the use of short (20–30 minutes) discrete tasks as a means of assessing potential and actual leadership and teamworking skills. Again this became prominent during the early 1940s and was typified by the sort of tasks run by the War Office Commissions Board selecting candidates for officer training. These consist of short problem-solving tasks requiring some physical ability; they are set to a group of four to eight participants, a leader is nominated (or they are briefed that it is a leaderless task), and given a time frame to operate in. Each candidate is then assessed by an observer against various criteria, which form the basis for selection. This has proved to be an enduring system and still forms part of the selection system for all three armed forces; and it is also used internally, for example as part of the selection process for 'fast-tracking' junior

* As a personal comment on the effectiveness of this type of training, I as a young officer took part in or led many such expeditions, and there is absolutely no doubt in my mind that these experiences were a tremendous help in dealing with some of the hazardous experiences I later encountered.

NCOs. The high level of accuracy of the system is testified to by the low drop-out rates from the training establishments, none of which are known for their low standards. From assessment for selection to assessment with a view to subsequent training or coaching was a small step and quickly made, both militarily and commercially.

The final contribution made by the forces is a particular tool that can be used within a programme, the high ropes course, which has been in military use since the last century. It is used as an individual confidence builder for which it is very effective. There have been some very creative programmes based on ropes courses, and they appear to be experiencing a resurgence in popularity.

So far we have discussed two of the influences on outdoor training, the original outward bound type programme and the armed forces; there is however another equally important influence that we have yet to discuss: the tremendous advances made over the last 20 years on a practical level in the study of human behaviour. Communication, change processes, management theory, how teams work, creativity, coaching theory, counselling – a quick look at the bookshelf beside my desk would reveal books on all these and many more, including strategy (western and oriental), quality circles, visualisation, Gestalt therapy, transactional analysis, neuro-linguistic programming, the theories of Moshe Feldenkrais and so on. With the huge increase in the number of tools and models available to modern trainers (as opposed to their counterparts 20 years ago) has come the ability to deal with much more subtle and complex issues.

These then are the major influences on current outdoor training: the original Outward Bound programme, which demonstrated the effectiveness of the outdoors as a tool for personal development; the use of this type of programme by the forces to focus on and develop specific leadership and team skills; the development of short discrete tasks to provide information about the current levels of leadership and teamworking skills for individuals and groups; and then finally the development of the wide range of models, tools and techniques which are now available to the trainer, and which can be used to extract, process and then put to use the information generated by the outdoors.

The learning cycle

The keystone that ties them together into a functional whole is a variation on Kolb's Learning Cycle. I have yet to come across an outdoor training organisation that does not subscribe to this concept in some form or other.

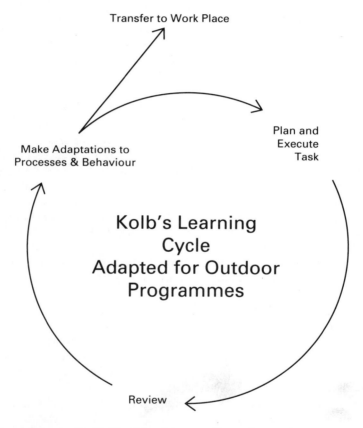

1. A team or individual is given a task to plan and carry out.
2. Having completed it they then review how they operated, the processes they used and how they affected the outcome, and also (if relevant) individuals' patterns of behaviour.
3. They then make adaptations to these processes and patterns of behaviour in order to make them more effective in achieving

successful and positive outcomes; these can then be tried out in a subsequent task.

Throughout this process the participants are encouraged to make connections and draw parallels in terms of behaviour and processes back at the workplace.

The process is cyclical and in the course of a programme participants would move through the process several times.

Different types of programme

These then are the elements that make up an outdoor programme, the variety of programmes offered as such being reflected in the origins of the medium. On the one hand you have the traditional outward bound type of programme, which offers broad-based personal developmental objectives, is task based with little formal review, and is likely to last 8–14 days. Alternatively you might have a two-hour task to illustrate a specific area (eg negotiation skills) as part of a much longer indoor-based programme, where anything up to a day might be spent reviewing the information generated, in light of the remainder of the programme. Then there is the middle ground, a three- or four-day programme focusing on a specific skill (eg team management techniques, or cultural change), with the time spent on review (as opposed to tasks) taking 40–60 per cent of the time available.

In terms of distinguishing between different programmes or designing your own programmes the factors to consider are:

- **Objectives:** are they to be broad focus developmental, or narrow focus on specific issues or skills?
- **Task vs Review:** how is the time going to be split between task and review and what is most appropriate in terms of the objectives?
- **Review Style:** it is unlikely that either a totally pedagogic or totally anagogic style is appropriate; it is likely that a blend of styles will fit a programme more effectively, but where and how to blend them needs to be defined.

7

For the remainder of this book I am going to talk about the type of outdoor programmes that I consider to be effective and commercially viable today. Using the criteria listed above I would characterise them as follows:

- **Objectives:** specific, focused on issues and skills relevant to the work environment.
- **Task vs review:** for specific objectives the reviews need to be focused, and hence facilitated by a trainer. Review time is likely to take between 40–60 per cent of the total time.
- **Review style:** with specific objectives there will certainly need to be some direction in terms of where to focus the review sessions, perhaps with some latitude if other major unexpected issues arise and need to be dealt with/cleared. Once working in the objective areas it is likely that the style will be considerably more anagogic.

Programmes are unlikely to last more than four or five days, and might well consist of an outdoor task (or tasks) followed by review as part of a larger indoor programme.

Safety considerations

Before closing this chapter there is one other major area that I feel is important to discuss. Anyone who has been involved in outdoor training for any length of time will have had to think carefully about the issue of using what are potentially dangerous activities to achieve work-related training objectives. In the context of the armed forces there is some justification for the element of danger, in as much as dealing with dangerous situations is a well publicised part of the job specification, but the subject does not fall within the parameters of this book.

The same potential justification however cannot apply outside that environment. A supervisor on a factory floor, a secretary or manager in an office, a salesman on his rounds, all have a moral and legal right to expect any work-related activities to be safe. Very few of them will have relevant training or experience of the outdoors, and it is likely that there will be some individuals who do not wish to be on the programme and are only attending because of real or perceived pressure from their superiors.

In order to deal with this I have formed a set of basic assumptions which I apply to any programme I become involved with, and offer them here not as definitive guidelines but to illustrate the issues involved:

- No commercial training objective can justify actual risk to the participants or staff involved in a programme.
- A provider of outdoor training has an obligation to look after each participant's (and trainer's) physical and mental wellbeing throughout a programme, and to ensure that at no time is anyone put in a situation, indoors or outdoors, which they feel unable to handle.
- The participants have a responsibility to tell a member of staff if they feel they are being placed in such a situation.
- When working with groups the trainer should not raise issues which he or she is not competent enough or sufficiently experienced to deal with, or which cannot be resolved satisfactorily within the context of the programme and its follow-up.

I hope these are all reasonably self-explanatory; in any case, they will be discussed in more detail later on.

What Can the Outdoors Offer My Organisation?

We know that

The outdoors as a training medium is not the answer to every people-related training need, as various providers have in the past suggested it might be – indeed I do not believe any single training medium is. It is however an exceptionally useful tool in the trainer's toolbox when it comes to addressing such training needs.

Why it is so useful

This chapter will look at why it is such a useful tool, and what it can offer an organisation. The reasons why it is so useful are best highlighted by describing the differences that distinguish it from other more conventional training media addressing similar areas:

Real experience

The outdoors is an environment where tasks are real, and failure and success bring real consequences. Intelligent task design means that specific issues can be highlighted in a fresh and new environment. Participants can practise teamwork and leadership, try out different ways of operating and behaving, and get immediate feedback from trainers and peers. They can then make modifications based on this feedback and try again. If for example there are communication issues between two teams at work, they can be given a task where success will require a lot of communication, and the review can be structured to focus on this area. Afterwards they can be given a different task (still requiring the same level of communication, or even raising it) to see if the changes have worked, and more importantly if they can be applied in the workplace.

Different environment

Working in a different and unfamiliar or new environment highlights patterns of behaviour which might otherwise pass unnoticed in a more conventional environment. It also makes for a steeper learning curve, since unusual and unforeseen circumstances tend to nullify habitual responses and encourage the participants to think again, and produce more original and considered responses.

'Safe' experimentation

We have already talked about teams trying out new ways of operating: the outdoors also offers a 'safe' arena in which they really can be tested, since any failures resulting from this experimentation will have no direct consequences financially or otherwise back in the real world. This is also true, provided experimentation is recognised for what it is, on a personal level.

Trust

One of the consequences of a team taking on an outdoor task of which they have no previous experience and which has real consequences, is the highlighting of trust and mutual support. This can be further highlighted if the outdoor staff take overt responsibility for the physical aspects of safety, apparently leaving the participants to concentrate on the interpersonal aspects, support and encouragement. This can generate high levels of mutual support, respect and trust, not often experienced in a business environment.

Impact

A properly designed outdoor programme will be aimed at a level which suits the physical abilities of the participants and will generate experiences which fully engage the attention of each participant and are truly memorable. If properly handled in review these memories can be used to key specific learning points for each individual participant, so that in the future whenever an analogous situation crops up he or she will associate it with that experience and the consequent learning. A simple example is rock climbing or abseiling: these can be used as part of an exercise looking at barriers and self-confidence. The feeling of success, elation and self-confidence usually generated by abseiling down a cliff face for the first time is truly memorable and by a process of association can be used to generate similar feelings when faced with barriers and lack of self-confidence in the workplace. Obviously such an exercise must be designed so that an individual who chooses not to abseil or climb is not placed under pressure to do so, and has a worthwhile contributory role to play as part of the overall exercise.

Fun

I have often heard it said that learning should be fun, and the outdoors offers more opportunities than most to make it so. The variety of activities available, along with the informal and relaxed atmosphere generated on a programme, can combine to generate an enjoyable learning experience. Furthermore a sense of play can encourage and support a sense of exploration, and a willingness to try out different or new options.

Motivation

The total impact of the factors listed above will often result in the participants returning to the workplace highly motivated. This is a resource that can then be utilised to aid the implementation of the changes generated by the programme.

Another way to express what an outdoor programme offers the participants is to look at it as an opportunity to take part in, and experience, a series of real-life parables of their work environment. These parables are involving, interactive, very memorable, enjoyable and (if properly designed) highly relevant to participants' current work situation. The icing on the cake is that after having experienced each of these parables, they can have the opportunity to sit down with the rest of the group and a facilitator, to discuss their experiences within the parable, and the implications of those experiences in the wider context.

To my mind the key advantage of this medium over any others currently available is the level of involvement, participation and enthusiasm it generates in the participants, which in turn means than any behavioural changes, learning, solutions to problems, courses of action, or organisational and cultural changes generated by such a programme are going to be relevant and, if properly handled, transferable back to the work environment.

This then is why an outdoor programme works; the next area to explore is what sort of skills and issues can be addressed using such a programme.

The skills and issues addressed

Any training or development programme is concerned with producing changes, whether on a micro level, in terms of how people carry out certain tasks, or a macro level, changing the structure or culture of an organisation, and persuading its members to buy into (and then adapt to fit) the new status quo. I hope it has become apparent that outdoor training is all about change; with imaginative design you can explore, and in most cases address, any issue or skill that involves looking at individuals or groups, and how they behave and interact. However by itself an outdoor programme is rarely enough, and there will need to be support from within the organisation to promote and encourage the changes generated by such a programme. We will explore this in more detail in the chapter on needs analysis and objective setting.

What follows is a short and obviously not definitive list of some of the areas where outdoor programmes have been used successfully to develop skills and address issues.

Leadership and management

This is perhaps one of the two most common focuses for a programme, and they have been run at every level from senior apprentices through supervisors and graduates to junior, middle and senior managers.

Teambuilding and team effectiveness

This is the other major focus for programmes: working with newly formed teams, helping them to establish ground rules and basic processes, then coaching them to help them start performing effectively; alternatively working with existing teams, looking at their internal and external processes and relationships and helping them make adjustments so that they can enhance their existing performance.

Multicultural teambuilding

Working with teams from diverse cultures, helping them to establish mutually acceptable patterns of behaviour, common agreed standards, and effective group processes, then coaching them for performance.

Organisational and culture change

Typically working with an organisation that has flattened its organisational pyramid, changed to a matrix type organisation, or been involved with major redundancies, or perhaps a combination of these. It is likely that a substantial part of the organisation is unsure of its future, does not understand what is going on, and distrusts the motives and actions of the management. In short, communication and trust are at a low when they are of paramount importance. One way to deal with these issues effectively is to run a series of outdoor programmes focusing on building trust and communication, with each group attending being a vertical slice of the organisation, eg a senior manager, a couple of junior managers, some supervisors, and a shift from the shop floor. In the course of the programme the levels of trust and communication are built up. In order to maintain this, the transfer mechanism at the end of the programme needs to involve a mechanism for maintaining communication levels in the workplace after the programme, so that issues can be quickly addressed before they become critical. On one programme on which I have worked this took the form of a video produced by the participants raising their concerns and fears; this went directly to the Managing Director who came down to the shop floor to answer them, and thereafter held regular open briefing sessions at which any employee could table questions and query the answers.

An alternative strategy for cultural change is 'cascading', where the change process is initiated by running a programme for staff at the top of the organisational pyramid, and this is then repeated on successively lower levels until the bottom level is reached. This is effective in an open and positive organisation, but less so in one where these qualities are in doubt.

Developing 'learning organisations'

This is a particular aspect of organisational and cultural change for which the outdoors is very effective. The whole structure of the programme demonstrates in a very clear and uncomplicated manner the learning process: experience, review, adaptation, application, and back around the cycle. As a programme progresses it is a simple matter to hand over the responsibility for managing and applying this cycle to the participants; it then only remains to build into the transfer element of the programme a mechanism whereby this can be continued (and initially monitored and coached) in the workplace. A very powerful direct application of the outdoors.

Integrated programmes

Here an outdoor programme becomes an element of a larger programme focused on any of the areas described in this list. For example: a ten-day programme looking at the theory of management might involve a three-day element containing a number of tasks designed to illustrate the theories and provide discussion material for the remainder of the programme. The variety of ways by which outdoor tasks and review processes can be integrated into other programmes is enormous and still being explored. Some of the most creative ones I have been involved with have been events where an organisation has combined a product launch with an event aimed at breaking down regionalisation within its sales force and building trust and communication between its members. The terminology used in the tasks and the outcomes reinforced details of the product, whilst the tasks themselves (and the reviews) focused on trust, mutual support, and communication.

Catalytic programmes

This often takes the form of a short programme prior to, or more effectively as part of, an important planning or decision-making conference. Around the meetings are timetabled tasks and reviews that focus on particular skills and issues that are significant to the main agenda; these might involve communication skills, creative thinking, developing strategies, negotiation and so on. These serve to highlight significant areas, encourage creative and original solutions, maintain interest and enthusiasm in the main agenda, and stimulate the participants.

Induction programmes

If an organisation already has a series of outdoor programmes running, managers often see them as an ideal way of introducing a new employee to the company, allowing them to rapidly become acquainted with the company culture, and to quickly form relationships with other employees.

Interpersonal and personal skills

It would be rare to devote an entire programme to a specific skill but tasks are often designed as part of a programme to focus on a particular skill. A comprehensive list would be huge; however some of the more common ones would include:

Clear communication	Motivating
Listening skills	Coaching
Delegating	Planning
Creative thinking	Negotiation
Co-ordinating	Financial management
Developing strategies	Passing on information
Building trust	Dealing with conflict
Problem solving	Managing resources

and many more . . .

Others

This list is not definitive, and really is a description of areas in which I have had substantial experience. I have also come across programmes focused on issues relating to Total Quality Management, which were run as part of a supervisors' programme, or in relation to NVQ's and so on. The list is always growing, and to my mind the only criterion that should affect this is the effectiveness of the programmes offered.

Finally I should point out that the items in this list are not mutually exclusive: a team effectiveness programme can also focus on management skills for particular individuals, and a catalytic programme can also focus on teambuilding. A feature of many of the programmes that I work on is that individuals highlight particular areas they wish to develop and set themselves objectives in relation to them; these are then addressed during the course of the programme, and progress is reviewed at the end of it.

The original question that started this chapter asked: 'What can the outdoors offer my organisation?' So far I have described the benefits it offers which distinguish it from other training media, and outlined the sort of areas and issues that can be addressed using the outdoors. However to be of any use there are still two questions to be answered:

1. Can the learning from an outdoor programme be effectively transferred to the workplace?
2. Are the results measurable?

The answers to both questions is undoubtedly yes, and they will be dealt with in detail in subsequent chapters.

3

Defining the Objectives

The first key element to running a successful outdoor programme is having well-defined and clear objectives; this is true of any training programme but doubly so of the outdoors. Here you are usually operating in areas where the measurements of success are likely to be at least partially subjective, and where achieving transferability to the workplace has historically been considered difficult to prove. I am not particularly impressed by this notion since, as I will describe later on in this chapter, it is a simple process to measure the results of an outdoor programme in such a way as to leave both the clients and providers in no doubt as to its success or failure, and I feel that perhaps the issue has not been the difficulty in assessing results, but unwillingness to subject programmes to this process.

Training needs analysis

However, before we look at defining and measuring objectives we need to look at the previous stage of the process and relate that to the use of the outdoors. Training needs analysis is a large subject, and not one I propose to deal with in detail here; Frances and Roland Bee offer an excellent introduction in *Training Needs Analysis and Evaluation* (IPM, 1994). However, I do intend to look at some areas that are often relevant when considering the use of outdoor training.

At an organisational level the process of change can be perhaps most simply illustrated as follows:

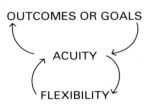

18

Initially a set of outcomes or goals are developed, describing a desired organisational structure, culture, and method of operation. These are usually developed at board level and are hopefully the result of long-term strategy and proactive responses to anticipated changes in the market.

The next stage is to look carefully at the organisation and decide exactly what the current state of play is: what skills already exist, what the current culture is, how the organisation functions and what resources are available within it. I use the word acuity here to convey the idea of a clear, factual, unemotional and uninfluenced view with no bias or unconscious prejudice.

Finally there is the process of deciding what changes are needed to achieve the outcomes and goals, which requires flexibility. These changes can be organisational: for example changing from a hierarchical, segmented company structure to a matrix structure, or flattening the organisational pyramid, or introducing quality circles. They can be cultural: any organisational changes will require a different way of behaving from the people involved. Then there is the personal level: individuals will almost certainly need different skills to fit into the new culture and organisation; these will range from work-based skills to interpersonal skills, and are likely to require training or education to develop them.

This is a continuous process, as interventions are made through training, structural change to the organisation, and other media, to move the company closer to the desired outcomes. It is unlikely that any one set of changes will move the organisation exactly to the desired outcome, as usually it is a process of continuous fine tuning, where a series of adjustments is made before achieving the desired result. The process is further complicated by the fact that the outcomes are not likely to remain static; more commonly these will be changing as the market changes, so effectively the company is actually trying to produce an organisation and culture that most effectively deals with current conditions, but is already changing to meet the conditions likely to prevail in subsequent years.

Implementing this process is a complex task; one of the tools used is training, and I perceive training needs analysis to be defining the training needed to help implement this process. This is the scenario against which outdoor programmes focused on culture change and organisational development are often set, and it raises several issues:

- To be recognised as successful any programme involved in the change process must have very clear and well-publicised objectives.
- Further, if the programme is to be credible, the evaluation must contain some objective measurements of effect, as otherwise it is possible to attribute the changes brought about by it to a wide variety of other causes.
- Looking at organisations as self-perpetuating organisms, they are by their nature resistant to change, and hence any change developed by such a programme will have to be actively encouraged and supported from the top of the organisation, if it is to survive its initial implementation.
- Outdoor programmes, because of their experiential nature, can be designed to address a number of issues simultaneously, eg culture change, team management techniques, and problem-solving and communication skills. So if correctly used they can be invaluable in this process.

Considered at an individual level, the question of resistance to change becomes very significant. The two questions usually asked in any training needs analysis are: what skills are important in your job, and what skills do you need training in? These are intelligent questions since they highlight the priorities of the individual within the role and the areas in which such training is likely to be welcomed. So an area that crops up in the answer to both is likely to be useful and one in which training will be enthusiastically received.

This may be acceptable to an organisation which provides goods or services, has considerable experience, and is operating in a static market. However, for a relatively new organisation, or one based in a changing market, I do not think that it is sufficient. There is a third question that should be asked: what skills in your job are encouraged and rewarded by the organisation? This then generates a much fuller picture, which is illustrated by the model below:

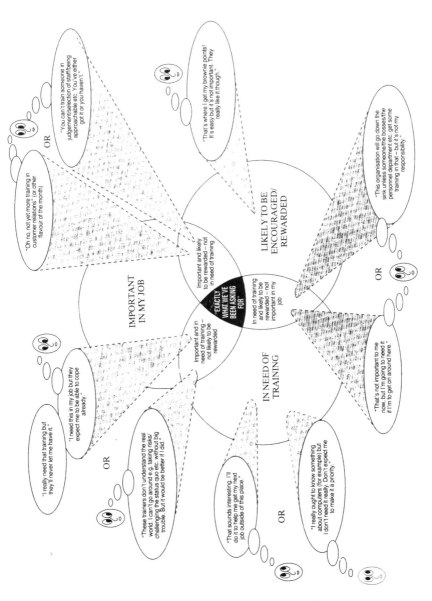

Illustration: © Sheppard Moscow Ltd, from Jill Fairbairns, 'Plugging the gap in training needs analysis', *Personnel Management*, February 1991.

Any training that falls outside the central area overlapped by all three circles is likely to meet with some form of resistance. Certainly any programmes involved in cultural or organisational change will need to be carefully handled if they are not to fall outside. The most common problem is for there to be a perception on the part of the participants that any changes that arise as a result of such a programme will not be encouraged or supported by their peers or managers. This should be a relatively simple problem to address, but the number of times I have encountered it suggests otherwise. It requires two actions: publicised support from the management structure emanating from the top, and education, explaining the aims and goals of the programme.

Programmes aimed at developing individuals or teams are also prone to the same problem. A team which has spent three or four days away developing more effective methods of operating, is likely to find considerable resistance from the teams and individuals they interact with, and they will need to be very robust, or receive considerable support, if they are to be effective in implementing these changes.

Eventually in the needs analysis process, outcomes are going to be developed for individuals and teams within the organisation. For example, if the organisation is flattening its pyramid, it is likely that supervisors and junior managers are going to have to take on more responsibility and be more proactive in their approach to problem solving* and teams are going to take on wider roles, sharing resources and liaising more with teams in other locations. Particular skills might well be highlighted as important to the future of the organisation, eg negotiation and communication, problem solving and so on. Finally there will almost certainly be some 'history' to deal with, which usually will consist of previous operating patterns which are no longer productive, hierarchical communication and decision-making processes, strict boundaries between different roles, and so on.

---

* I mentioned earlier, when describing the origins of outdoor training, how the armed forces had been compelled to deal with the way in which the decision-making level had moved down the hierarchy to the corporals. My experience is that a similar but often unrecognised process has been happening for some time in industry.

The design process

It is at this stage that decisions are made as to how to effect these outcomes and what media to use, and it is here that the design process for developing and delivering outdoor programmes starts, as the outcomes mentioned above can all be influenced by outdoor programmes. The first stage of the design process is to turn them into tightly defined objectives, and the definitions I find most useful are:

Specific

The objective needs to be very specific, focusing on a particular issue or skill. 'Improving communication skills' to my mind is not an adequate objective. I would want to know what skill we are talking about, eg listening, giving feedback, briefing etc. I would also want to know in which circumstances it becomes important, and between what levels, eg between supervisors and their teams, or between supervisors and managers at meetings. All this is extremely relevant to the design process.

Measurable

There needs to be a way of measuring the result or the effect of the programme and this means that for each objective there need to be a number of criteria by which improvement or its lack can be measured. With imagination it is possible to devise criteria for almost any objective. A simple example might focus on management skills in supervisors, where an effective way to assess the effect of a programme would be to run an appraisal of the supervisors before the programme, and then to run a second, two to three months later. A more complex example might focus on improving and broadening the flow of information and ideas between supervisors and managers; here a number of criteria might be used such as the length of weekly meetings between the two, the agenda discussed, the individuals' opinions, the measure of downward flow of information, and so on.

Another point to make is that these are all comparisons, and in order to make an effective determination of the changes produced by the programme they need to be measured both before and after the programme. This process also forms a vital part of the post-course evaluation process, of which more later.

Achievable

Opinions vary as to what and how much can actually be achieved within the space of a short programme. I have in the past been presented with a list of objectives for a three-day programme which covered the complete range of management skills, a major element of teambuilding, and several company-specific issues. The participants were all newly promoted to supervisory posts, with no previous supervisory experience. When I asked for the list to be prioritised, the reaction was that all items were important. Further, investigating the company-specific issues highlighted the fact that, in order for two of them to be resolved, specific action was going to be needed from the company, and this would not be likely to happen for at least six months. As matters stood, the objectives were not achievable, as firstly, the range of skills and issues to be addressed was too great for the time available, secondly it was too ambitious for the participants' role, and thirdly, two of the issues could not be addressed at all within the context of the programme, since any resolution reached would have been lost by the time action was taken by the company concerned. After a great deal of discussion and analysis, we eventually compromised on a four-day programme focusing specifically on supervisory skills, developing effective work teams, and one of the company-specific issues.

Relevant

It is very easy, when designing a programme, to get carried away and start designing in tasks and reviews to focus on issues that are not relevant to the objectives. Often it is a case of knowing when to stop. On one occasion I was working with another consultant designing a teambuilding programme where the teams were multinational, were being formed at the start of the programme, and were going to operate for three to four months carrying out a research and consultancy role within their own organisation. The objectives were clearly defined, and can be summarised simply as giving them the tools and processes (bearing in mind the multicultural nature of the team) to function effectively and coherently as teams – or, as the project manager put it 'to hit the ground running'. After two hours working on this, we found ourselves designing elements into the programme which would prejudge not only how those team members would collect the information for the research, but also how it would then be organised and dealt with. Clearly this was beyond the objectives we had been given and was potentially damaging to the overall project.

Time related

Any set training objective should be time related, and in the case of the outdoors there seems to be a general consensus that the time to check on implementation or transfer of learning is between four and twelve weeks. This time span is dictated by two elements: firstly, the time it takes for learning to be implemented in the workplace, and for it to be recognised and accepted by the hierarchy and peers; secondly, the length of time new behaviour is likely to last without support from them. As a personal view I think the ideal situation is a two-stage monitoring process. The first comes after two or three weeks, when the initial euphoria has worn off and it is possible to identify where there is adequate support, and where it is lacking. It is then possible to remedy this lack while memories and motivation are still fresh from the programme. The second stage should then happen after about eight weeks, as by then any new behaviour should be assimilated into the workplace, and should be an accepted part of the culture. Its effect can then be looked at, and compared with that defined in the programme's objectives. The results of this comparison can then form part of the programme evaluation.

Supported

I have already talked about this, but it is fundamental to achieving real change in the workplace, and lack of support is perhaps the most common problem encountered when dealing with outdoor programmes. The vast majority of organisations are unconsciously resistant to change, and to implement change as an individual or a team within an organisation can be a very difficult process. For example, if a junior manager goes on a programme learning about alternative styles of management, and as a result makes some changes to her own style, she is going to encounter a number of barriers to implementing them in the workplace. Implementing changes is likely to upset the status quo, and her manager is going to want performance to be maintained while these changes are being put in place. (So is she if her pay is performance related.) The supervisors who report to her are going to be sceptical, and again unwilling to risk not achieving targets; in addition, they then have to sell these changes down the line, and do not have the advantage of having been on the programme. It is likely that she will meet with a negative response from many of her peers, who have either already had a bad experience, or who feel threatened by the changes and her enthusiasm for implementing them. Finally, there are the administrative processes that might have to be changed to accommodate these changes. To overcome such barriers a considerable amount of motivation, determination and enthusiasm is needed, and in the situation outlined above (which is based on real experience), it is likely that many individuals would not achieve any real change.

The case for providing ongoing support and encouragement for individuals and teams in the workplace after an outdoor programme is clear. Unfortunately, in my experience it is also one of the most likely areas to be overlooked. The problem can be resolved in several ways, and the suggestions given below can be adapted to apply to teams as well as individuals:

- A support system can be set up for her when she returns, or at the very least her manager must be briefed by the training department on the likely outcomes of such a programme, and his support enlisted. He in turn can then provide support and encouragement when it comes to overcoming the other barriers. His aid can also be enlisted when it comes to monitoring the outcomes; this allows him to become involved and play a positive part in the process, and at the same time he can remain aware of the issues that might be being generated.
- In a similar vein it may be appropriate for the supervisors to

be briefed on the likely outcomes of such a programme, and their support and perhaps active participation enlisted, before they are effectively presented with a *fait accompli*. When doing this care must be taken not to generate false or unreal expectations, which if not met would cause negativity.

- A network can be set up, of people who have already been on such a course, and who have already encountered the problems and so can suggest ways of overcoming them. On programmes it is often suggested that participants use each other in this way when they get back to the workplace.

- As already discussed, the monitoring process (especially the two-stage one described in the previous section) can itself provide a forum for support and encouragement.

- The entire organisation can be sent on such a programme. In culture change programmes aimed at organisations, where the changes required are major and affect large parts of the company, this often happens. In as short a time as is commensurate with financial and business constraints, the entire organisation is cycled through an outdoor programme, operating in groups comprising vertical slices of the company (a senior manager, some junior managers, some supervisors and a shift from the shop floor). Everyone is then tuned it to the proposed changes, and has a stake in implementing them.

- Counselling is a service increasingly offered by organisations as part of their employee support systems, and again can provide a useful source of support.

These then are the criteria to apply to defining course objectives. Taken together, they allow you to define the exact outcomes you wish to achieve; they allow you to set up (and agree) clear measurable success criteria by which the programme's effectiveness can later be judged; they ensure that these are achievable within the context of the programme; they also ensure that they are relevant and in tune with the goals of the organisation; and finally they ensure that they are supported and encouraged from within the organisation.

Setting up and defining the objectives in this way is to my mind one of the critical stages in producing a successful programme. When this process is carried out, any ambiguity concerning exactly what is expected from the programme is dealt with, as the provider knows exactly what is expected in terms of outcomes, and the clients are clear on what they need to provide, in terms of support, if they are to maintain and promote these outcomes within their organisation. It is the basis on which the remainder of the design and delivery process rests. The next stage in this process is structuring a programme to meet these objectives.

4

Structuring A Programme

The structure is the framework of processes, each of which forms an essential and integral part of the complex system that makes up an outdoor programme. Many of these processes are interlinked, or work as elements within larger processes, which then themselves form part of the larger framework. An awareness of these processes, what they achieve and how they work, is often a major factor in the successful outome of a programme. This chapter identifies the key issues that define the requirements for these processes, and suggests a system which in my experience is extremely effective, and is flexible enough to be applied to a programme looking at any of the objectives so far discussed.

The issues we will look at include:

- the basic assumptions which form the foundation for outdoor training
- the learning process
- physical and emotional welfare and safety, including confidentiality and reports, personal and group outcomes, dealing with the hidden agenda, cultural and gender issues
- task design
- review process and design
- transfer to work.

Task design, the review process and design, and transfer to work, all merit separate chapters, but I now intend to focus on the others.

Basic assumptions

The 15 years' experience of outdoor training programmes on which this book is based spans a broad spectrum, ranging from some of the more rigorous military development and selection programmes, through outward bound types, to present-day

29

commercial programmes similar to those described in this book. In each case I was initially a participant or trainee, and later became involved in their design and delivery. For the last six years I have focused almost exclusively on designing and delivering commercial programmes for a very broad range of organisations, from all sectors of industry and public service. Over this period I have consistently tried to define a simple philosophy or set of operating assumptions which enable me to run programmes that are positive learning experiences for the participants, commercially effective, and ethical. (If ethical seems to be an unusual word in this context its meaning will soon become clear.) Starting on a fairly broad front, there are four fairly general principles I operate from, and many of the specific assumptions are derived from these.

1. *Each individual sees, hears, feels, interprets and reacts to the world around him- or herself uniquely.*
This is a more precise way of saying that everybody is different. Practically every trainer I know would agree with this; however, many do not take it into account when dealing with groups.

2. *In people-related issues, there is very rarely a black and white solution.*
This follows directly from the first point. Since each people-issue is unique there is no such thing as a single, across-the-board solution applicable every time an issue surfaces; there are likely to be a number of different solutions ranging across the spectrum, one of which will be most appropriate to that particular group of people.

3. *Taking responsibility for oneself and the consequences of one's actions is a desirable goal towards which to move.*
The concept of development implies a process of self-directed change. To be workable, this requires the above belief. The alternative is a fatalistic mind-set in which things are pre-ordained, which completely nullifies the process.

4. *A commercial training programme is an extension of the workplace.*
Basically a programme does not operate in limbo, but has real consequences in terms of people's futures, success, financial circumstances, and welfare, in the workplace. Therefore a trainer

facilitating a teambuilding programme has always to be aware of the long-term effects of his or her actions and their consequences. For example, during a teambuilding programme there is often a stage in the process when the team is quite negative and fragmented, before roles and responsiblities are defined and agreed. It would be extremely counter-productive to allow a team to return to the workplace without their having resolved and moved on from this stage, and it would have real consequences for the team members in terms of their future within that company. It is the trainer's role to ensure that this state of affairs does not happen. This may seem an obvious point to make, but it is surprising how often it is lost amidst trainers' and managers' discussions of how teams and individuals 'should' and 'should not' behave, and their attempts to achieve this magical state. Further, in the participants' eyes the programme is simply another part of their work, and unless they are told otherwise they will quite reasonably expect similar standards of health and safety, conditions of work and rules of behaviour to be operating.

From these general principles I have derived the basic assumptions or rules that form an integral part of the structure I use on outdoor programmes. They are as follows:

1. *No commercial training course warrants real risk to the participants, and the provider has a responsibility to take all reasonable precautions to ensure that this does not happen.*
By real risk I mean physical danger in terms of injury or death, and in this respect the outdoor element of a programme should be run with the same safety standards as any other commercial organisation involved in training in a potentially hazardous environment. I would define the word injury as anything beyond a scratch, bruise or minor pulled muscle. It is not possible to guarantee that someone will not suffer this sort of minor injury whilst working outdoors. However a good provider is always looking to minimise the odds of this, and anything beyond it is unacceptable, and would warrant investigation.

Apart from the purely ethical viewpoint, the commercial cost to a company of losing an employee for a week or two can be exorbitant. Safety is a major issue and will be referred to again, both later in this chapter, in terms of setting up a physical 'safety net', and in the chapters on task design and resourcing.

31

2. *Within the context of a programme, no-one should be pressured into a situation or activity in which they do not wish to be involved.*

This reflects two principles: again safety, in terms of giving people a choice whether or not to participate in a particular aspect of the programme which they personally might feel is too demanding; secondly, this in turn hands over to the individual an element of decision-making and taking responsibility for him- or herself. The wording deliberately encompasses both outdoor and indoor situations, since in my experience, for some individuals reviews and associated sessions can generate equally as much tension and stress as outdoor activities. This also pre-empts another potential issue where an individual has strong preconceptions and/or previous negative experience, which can generate a lot of stress prior to a task. Declaring this assumption at the start of a programme defuses the situation, and the individual is simply asked to keep an open mind about the session or task until he or she has had a chance to see what is actually involved; then a decision can be made about what role, if any, he or she wishes to play. (An aspect of task design we will be discussing later is the provision of a variety of roles.)

3. *All participants have a responsibility to tell the staff if they feel they are being placed in a situation which they cannot, or do not wish to, deal with.*

Again this comes back to the two principles mentioned previously, regarding safety and taking responsibility. The 'safety nets' get their own sections later, but briefly: tasks are designed to be safe for participants to carry out; however outdoor staff are not mind-readers and it sometimes happens that participants unexpectedly find something too difficult, or a particular combination of circumstances causes a problem. By telling a member of staff, he or she then allows the staff to devise an alternative, or draw the attention of the group to the problem so that they can re-evaluate their plan, whichever seems the most appropriate.

4. *In terms of impact and memorability, learning is most effective when it is self-generated, by the individual or group.*

This is derived from observations made over the period of my involvement in using the outdoors as a medium for development.

The corollary is that this sort of learning or change of behaviour is only generated if the people themselves see the need. As a friend once said, you can lead a horse to water, but he will only drink if he is thirsty. This itself then starts to influence the way you design the tasks, and some of the issues involved.

5. *The trainers have a responsibility not to attempt to deal with or highlight issues that they do not have the expertise or facilities to cope with effectively.*
Here we are talking about consequences, just as in counselling, if an issue is raised which is beyond the counsellor's expertise to deal with, then it is referred to someone who has greater expertise in that area. When working on an outdoor programme the option of referring is not always present. It is therefore an unfortunate truth that an issue might be raised that cannot be dealt with. As a trainer, I deliberately avoid such issues unless the group raise them; but if they do, I acknowledge the issue along with the fact that I cannot deal with it. This in itself raises the issue of reporting back to the organisation either on individuals or groups; it has various ramifications and is discussed later in the section on the emotional 'safety net'.

These then are the basic principles and assumptions from which I operate. Effectively, they highlight the issues that in my experience have proved to be key in the use of the outdoors for commercial training. The major ones are:

- the issue of participants' emotional and physical safety
- the issue of participants being pressured by their employers, the providers or other group members into situations against their will
- the relevance and effectiveness of learning generated by the outdoors
- managing expectations with regard to how the programme is going to function and what the ground rules are, and to a lesser extent which issues can realistically be dealt with.

I would hope that these principles and operating assumptions will seem fairly obvious. They describe my response to the issues that have arisen while I have been involved in commercial outdoor programmes. I feel very strongly that anyone involved in an outdoor programme needs to be aware of these issues, to have thought through their consequences, and to be able to present a reasoned and ethical response to each of them. You may or may not agree with my responses, but the point is that you must have answers, which are ethically justifiable, and the people on your programme must be aware of what they are, so that they have a clear idea of exactly where they stand.

The learning process

I have already described the adaptation of Kolb's Learning Cycle which forms the basis of almost every commercial outdoor programme; it is shown in more detail on page 35.

In practice this becomes a repetitive cycle of task and review, with the review encompassing the elements of reflection, adaptation, and making connections to the workplace. (Whilst the reviews contribute to the transfer process, the actual mechanism for transfer is usually handled in a separate session at the end of the programme.) Around this cycle can then be fitted the issues or objectives of the programme.

First, however, it is necessary to flowchart these issues and objectives and then use the chart as a basis for designing the cycle of task and review. Rather than try to describe this process in theory, I give an actual example.

My initial involvement in this programme stemmed from a phone call in which I was asked if I could design and deliver a programme in Germany. The background was that BP were putting together a number of teams comprising 10–12 senior managers from all over Europe, and their brief was to take an internal consultancy role, looking at the horizontal systems and linkages between the different European divisions and suggesting ways that these might be more effectively managed. They were specifically looking at sharing best practice, simplification, and adding value; they had a time frame of about three months in which to operate; and it was envisaged that at least half of that time would be spent in gathering information around Europe. Each team had a specific area to concentrate

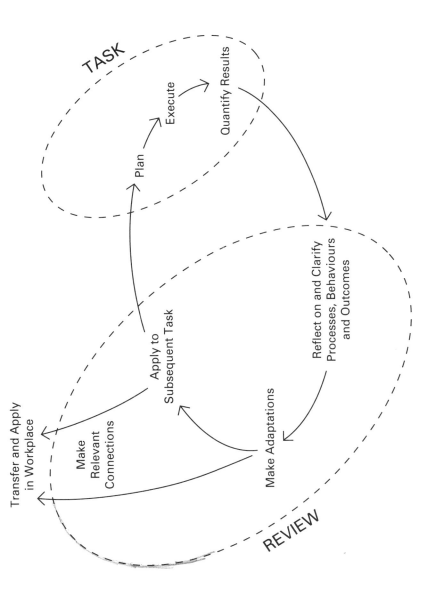

on, which involved a certain amount of specialised knowledge.

The brief for the outdoor programme was to provide a short, intensive teambuilding package, which would also start to emphasise the issues involved. There were two days available for the programme, the teams were likely to contain at least six different nationalities, and the operating language was to be English. In addition, whilst this programme was to be run for four teams in northern Germany, a similar programme was to be run in the UK by another organisation; and the two programmes had to match as closely as possible in terms of style, content, delivery and outcomes.

Two consultants from this organisation, John Campbell and Gary Edwards, met with me to plan the programmes jointly, and make sure they would match. The first step in the planning process was to define the issues or objectives which would be dealt with within the programme. Our list included:

- **teamworking skills:** listening skills, giving and receiving feedback, appropriate leadership styles, developing best practice within the team, and inter-team collaboration versus competition
- **multicultural team issues:** exploring and defining the teams' values, and creating a standard set of procedures which the whole team could relate to and use comfortably and effectively
- **sharing best practice:** looking at the issues involved in receiving and giving information, adding value, simplification, and sharing best practice.

We then flowcharted these issues to gain some idea of how, and in what order, we would address them with a suitable sequence of task and review. Because of the limited time available, the tasks had to be multi-focused or layered, so that the trainer reviewing could first of all look at how the team had been operating internally, and then later in the review switch to how they had interacted with the other teams around them. This meant more time spent in review. We eventually produced the flowchart shown below, which in its turn started to define the type of exercises needed.

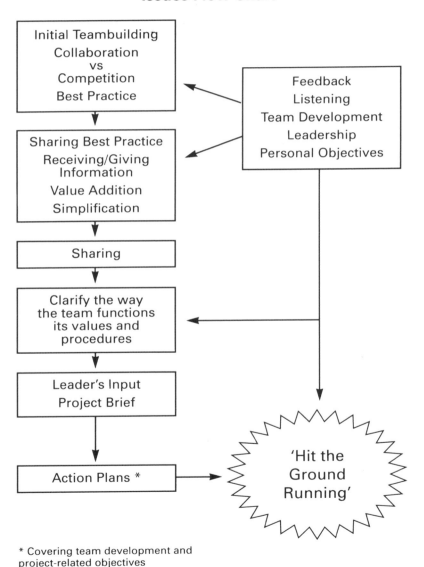

BPs Teambuilding Event
28–30 June 1992
Issues Flow Chart

* Covering team development and
project-related objectives

We felt that the first area to be addressed should be teambuilding, focusing on developing both the individual skills and group procedures, and values needed for each team to function effectively. The seniority of the people involved meant that it was likely that the process would be more one of adapting existing skills rather than learning new ones, and hence could be dealt with quite quickly. The focus was more likely to be on values and procedures. Next we felt that it was important to look at the issues involved in collaboration between teams, and how to deal with the problems it raised. We also felt it was important to highlight the negative consequences of competitive behaviour in their particular circumstances. Finally, with regard to the teambuilding element, we thought it important to introduce the concept of best practice, and highlight examples of it.

We then thought it was important to look at the people-issues related to sharing best practice in a multicultural environment, receiving and giving information, adding value and simplification. As part of that process we felt that it would be appropriate for the four teams to share with each other any learning and outcomes that they had so far achieved.

We decided that since time was a critical factor, throughout the programme the exercises used to focus on the issues would also be designed so that it would be possible, if necessary, to highlight the teamworking skills, feedback, listening skills, leadership and further team development issues within the reviews. We thought that at this stage it would be imperative to clarify the procedures and values each team had developed for itself, and then to emphasise and reinforce them.

The final element was for the team leaders to brief their teams on their specific task for the three months, and develop action plans to start the ball rolling.

We will return to the tasks and reviews in the relevant sections later. For the moment the point to hold on to is that by flowcharting the objectives or issues to be dealt with, you are already starting to define the content and structure of the programme, especially the tasks and reviews.

Safety net (physical)

I hope that one of the things which has already been strongly stressed is the responsibility of the provider to ensure that any task participants are asked to take part in as part of a training programme is completely safe.

There are several key areas to consider:

- competent outdoor staff
- serviceability, maintenance, and suitability of equipment
- task design
- checking the physical abilities and limitations of the participants
- providing a supportive environment, in which participants do not feel pressured into situations which they feel are beyond them, and are free to express this.

The first two areas will be looked at in a later chapter on resourcing programmes; the third has its own chapter; the rest of this section deals specifically with the remaining two areas.

The instructor's role

In any outdoor programme there are two areas of responsibility: one covering the outdoor elements of the programme, one the indoor. For convenience I will label them as the instructor's role and the trainer's role. Often an individual will carry out both in respect of a group he or she is working with, but in this section I want to focus on the instructor's role and the responsibilities it entails. These are:

1. To ensure the safety of the participants and trainers at all times, when they are taking part in, or observing, the tasks.
2. To run the tasks in such a way as to generate useful information for review.
3. Where necessary (no trainer can be in two places at once) to observe processes and behaviours within the group and report this information back to the trainer.

The first responsibility is the priority, but often in the context of programmes it is the least obvious, and so has to be emphasised strongly. One of the key areas here is the fitness level and medical health of the participants. Obtaining this information is vital, but there are various issues that can arise when doing so.

The first and most commonly encountered problem is declaration of health problems. Many people have health problems which they are unwilling to declare to their employers, because they feel it is likely to have an adverse affect on their careers. This can be a major problem and I have encountered in the past people who initially have not declared heart conditions, high blood-pressure, and other equally serious problems for this reason.

The second is interpretation: if a person goes to his or her GP for a medical check-up before going on an outdoor training programme, with no other information a doctor will quite correctly take the worst possible case in terms of the level of agility and fitness needed to take part safely, and use that as the benchmark when assessing that person's suitability. Using those criteria half the population would probably be considered unsuitable.

A third problem arises on occasion when employees show considerable reluctance to sign forms to do with medical matters. This is usually due to a combination of circumstances, concerns about signing disclaimers, reluctance to discuss health problems at all, and as a way of expressing negative emotions. For example, it is not unusual on culture change programmes for the participants to arrive with considerable unexpressed concerns, negativity and suspicions about the whole process.

Whatever the problems encountered, the instructor has a responsibility to make every sensible effort to obtain this information,and should not be willing to take responsibility for the participants' safety during tasks without it.

Over the last four years I have developed a questionnaire (see opposite) which I now use on every programme; it is designed to elicit the relevant information, whilst not triggering any of the problems mentioned above. It is sent out to the participants prior to the programme with a covering letter asking them to fill it in, and suggesting that if they are unsure about any of the questions, or have not had a recent check-up, they ask their doctor for help in filling it out. They are asked to bring the completed forms to the programme where one of the outdoor staff will collect and process them.

This to my mind covers most eventualities, and the only modifications I have had to make, so far, have been when dealing with significantly older participants or people with disabilities; here I have stipulated prior medical check-ups or have had to ask for more information about the implications of the disability.

Health Check Form

CONFIDENTIAL

The following information is for the use of the outdoor staff on the course only. It will not be communicated to your parent company, and it will only be used for administration and safety purposes.

Name:

Age:

1. Are you currently, or have you recently, been taking any form of medication?   YES/NO

2. Can you swim 40m in a swimming pool without touching the sides or the bottom?   YES/NO

3. Do you suffer from any of the following:
   - ○ Diabetes?   YES/NO
   - ○ Epilepsy?   YES/NO
   - ○ Asthma?   YES/NO
   - ○ Back problems?   YES/NO
   - ○ Heart problems or associated complaints?   YES/NO
   - ○ High blood-pressure?   YES/NO

4. Are you allergic to any medications?   YES/NO

5. Have you had any form of cold, flu or other viral infection in the last two months?   YES/NO

6. Do you have any form of physical disability, eg knees, shoulder, hips, etc?   YES/NO

7. Is there anything else that the staff running the outdoor part of the course should be aware of?   YES/NO

If you have answered 'YES' to any of these questions, please give further details below, and/or chat to one of the members of staff.

CONFIDENTIAL

You will see that the form is confidential between the outdoor staff and the participants, a fact which should be stressed repeatedly, both when it is distributed, and when it is collected in by the instructors. Secondly it is simple, requiring yes/no answers, and so there is likely to be little confusion in filling it out. Finally there is no requirement to sign it, so it does not raise barriers in that respect.

The instructor's attitude

This is the first link in the chain that makes up the safety system. The next link, and to my mind of equal importance, is the attitude and conduct of the instructors. We have already briefly defined their role, and its first priority, namely, ensuring the safety of participants and trainers during the task. If they are to be effective they must form a specific relationship with the participants, showing the following attitudes:

1. *Their role and its priorities must be clear.* As has been said about many other issues, there are only three things to remember about the instructor's role: safety, safety and safety.
2. *Competence and confidence.* Not only must they *be* competent in the outdoor environment but they must *appear* so, in order to inspire confidence in the participants.
3. *Trust.* The participants must feel able to trust the instructor to have their best interests at heart, and give them accurate, unbiased information. A classic example of how this can be broken down unnecessarily is where, as part of a task, the instructor has deliberately to mislead or lie to the participants; once this has happened the participants will automatically question his or her intentions every time he passes information, even when it is safety related. This is not acceptable, and therefore to my mind neither are tasks that involve deliberate deception.
4. *Circumspection.* The majority of instructors have led interesting and exciting lives, and the participants are usually interested in their backgrounds, often as a way of assessing their experience and competence. This can be very flattering, but there are few things more likely to cause problems than an

instructor telling a graphically hair-raising story about how he nearly died whilst abseiling off a mountain in a blizzard, as part of his briefing for a task involving abseiling. (This really happened, and the trainer spent most of the review dealing with the problems it caused rather than the task itself.)

5. *Level-headedness.* A common phenomenon on outdoor programmes is a sort of group euphoria or alternatively a type of 'failure hysteria'. In the first case the group are doing very well with a task and are getting carried away and over-confident; as the euphoria increases common sense tends to disappear and the group tends to forget the safety standards and rules they have been given. This is a very real and dangerous phenomenon, and in my experience the majority of injuries occur whilst groups are in this euphoric state. It is very easy for an instructor to get 'pulled' into the same state of mind, and it is vital that it does not happen, so that there is someone to pull the group up and point out what is happening. The second phenomenon, that of 'failure hysteria', is also fairly common and occurs when a group is very competitive and is failing badly in a task; a sort of hysteria takes over and anything is acceptable providing it might save the day. Almost always the first restrictions to be challenged are those concerning safety, and how they are 'excessive' and putting the group under an 'unfair' disadvantage. There is less tendency to get involved with the process, but correspondingly much more firmness is needed to point out what is happening to the group, and to maintain the standards. In either case level-headedness is an extremely important attribute, to avoid either being 'pulled' into the euphoria, or the temptation to give in and relax safety standards.

To summarise, a colleague of mine introduces the instructors to the group somewhat lightheartedly as follows: 'They are generally fairly quiet and easy-going individuals, so if you do hear one of them start to raise his voice, you had better stop what you're doing and listen carefully, because you're either about to do something that is potentially dangerous, or you've stolen his sandwiches, which on the whole is much the same thing.'

The ground rules

The final element of the safety net consists of the ground rules, several of which we have already mentioned in passing:

1. *Participants should not be pressurised into taking part in an activity which they feel is beyond their capability.*
Tasks are designed to be safe for people with normal capabilities and limits, and are then modified if necessary in the light of information generated by the health check forms. However there are always unforeseen problems: rarely it might be a medical condition the participant did not initially consider worth mentioning, or, more commonly, it is likely to be a particular fear or phobia. Whatever the reason, and aside from the principles we discussed earlier, it is clearly very detrimental to an individual's welfare for him or her to be pressured – by either an instructor or group of peers – into a situation which that individual feels he or she will not be able to deal with.

2. *Participants have a responsibility to inform the instructor if they feel that they are being asked to do something that is beyond them.*
This follows directly from the previous ground rule, and is particularly relevant when dealing with a fear or phobia. Speaking from personal experience, it is not always possible to tell from someone's behaviour or expression how close they are to their limits; it is therefore the participant's responsibility to tell the instructor if this is happening. Once this has come to light, it is then the group's responsibility to find an alternative method for completing the task, which does not involve that individual carrying out that particular activity; exceptionally the instructor might intervene and modify the task.

3. *The instructor has the right of veto.*
The instructor will of course be forming his own opinion about the above and will in any case intervene if he feels necessary. This most commonly happens when there is a lot of peer group pressure, or the particular individual feels that there is such pressure, usually mistakenly. In either case it calls for tactful but effective intervention by the instructor and a careful examination

of what the individual hopes to gain from completing the activity, as opposed to the stress and anxiety it is likely to cause him or her. The other common occasion when this becomes relevant is where individuals have unrealistic expectations of themselves in terms of their physical abilities, for example when planning an orienteering task which expects sedentary office staff to run three or four miles in half an hour, and so on. (Unfortunately, for the reasons already given, the instructor will sometimes use this veto unnecessarily, but that is infinitely preferable in terms of safety to not intervening at all.)

4. *The ultimate responsibility for safety is the instructor's and in this respect his or her word is final.*

It is very easy for a trainer to get carried away with the complexities of review and achieving objectives, and to start modifying tasks to help focus on particular areas. This is commendable, but I have often seen trainers get carried away and start to make modifications which marginally and perhaps unwittingly affect safety. This is not acceptable and it is the instructor's responsibility to ensure that this does not happen. Further, when a task involves more than one instructor supervising safety, it is imperative that each has clearly defined areas of responsibility, so that if something untoward does happen, the response can be effective and immediate, and not, as I have seen happen on one occasion, lead to a situation where three instructors stand looking at each other, each waiting for the other to veto a potentially dangerous course of action by an individual.

These then are the safety ground rules by which the instructors, trainers and participants operate on a programme; if they are to be effective then everybody on the programme needs to be aware of them.

We have talked about providing a physical safety net, and this is exactly how I view it: as a complex interweaving system with built-in backups, so that if one element fails to function there is an alternative element to replace it; thus tasks are designed to be safe with a range of roles to suit various abilities, participants have a choice about how they participate in them and to what level, and finally there is the instructor to monitor and supervise the whole process. Of necessity, and in accordance with the principles already described, there is an element of taking responsibility for one's own safety and welfare. However the fundamental principle is still that the provider is responsible for taking every reasonable precaution to look after the safety of participants and trainers alike.

Safety net (emotional)

A less considered aspect of outdoor training, but to my mind equally important, is the intensity of feeling and emotion which it can generate. In terms of learning and subsequent transfer this is a very positive element of the programme, but it does have to be very carefully handled to keep it so, and to ensure that the emotional welfare of the participants is not affected.

In order to do this there are several areas to consider:

- the role of the trainer
- guidelines for the review process
- confidentiality and reports
- personal and group outcomes
- hidden agenda
- culture and gender issues.

As with the issue of physical safety, the intention is to provide an interlocking or mutually supporting system, within which the trainer can operate effectively without generating any negativity, and if necessary can deal positively with emotional distress. Before I describe it I think it may be useful to describe briefly why it is necessary.

The review process is in essence a very simple one: after a task has been attempted by the group, the outcomes and the means by which these outcomes were achieved are first of all clarified, and then agreed, by the group and the trainer; these are then used as a basis from which to identify and reinforce effective and successful processes (best practice), and to identify and modify (or change) those which are not effective; finally there needs to be a commitment from the group to try out the modifications in a subsequent task.

There are various ways that this process can go astray, or be sabotaged from within the group. Louder or more forceful individuals can dominate and suppress quieter or less forceful ones, so that the latter's views and perceptions are not expressed and thus are lost. This not only results in inaccurate pictures of the behaviours and processes, but it can after a while alienate, or disenchant and demotivate, the quieter members of the group. In a similar vein, if there is no structure or format to the review, the process can also be disrupted by people who are not used to discussing issues in large groups, by interrupting, excessive repetition and lack of direction.

Individuals can often have their own agenda and values which they wish to impose on the group. Often tied in with this is the behaviour associated with 'game playing' as described by Eric Berne in his book *Games People Play*. This is usually a more subtle form of disruption, of which sometimes the individual concerned is unaware, but nonetheless it is often very disruptive, and needs to be dealt with quickly.

If a review is to be effective then on occasions there will be discussion, and hence feedback, about an individual's behaviour and how appropriate or effective it is. This can be stressful and/or threatening for both the person giving the feedback and the person receiving it, and can often generate a lot of emotion; in addition the style of delivery can often inadvertently exacerbate the problem. Exactly the same problems can occur when giving feedback to a group as opposed to an individual.

The existence of these potential problem areas makes clear the case for an 'emotional safety net'. This is best described by outlining the trainer's role, and giving a set of guidelines for participants. (I deliberately refer to them as guidelines because, unlike the ground rules for ensuring physical welfare, which are absolute, these guidelines are often modified to fit the intellectual level of the participants, and the issues likely to arise. Indeed, I occasionally outline some of the issues I have highlighted above to the participants, and ask them to generate their own guidelines, a process which is often very effective.)

The trainer's role

For the review process to be successful, the combination of role and guidelines must not only address potential problems, it must generate an open and supportive environment within which the review can take place; further, it must generate trust, both between the group and the trainer, and between the group members themselves. In order to generate this environment, and trust, the group will need to be clear exactly what the role of the trainer is.

The trainer's role is to guide the reviews so that they generate information and ideas that are likely to be relevant and useful to the programme's objectives. The information about how the group completed the tasks and how they experienced them will come from the participants themselves, but if the trainer feels that a relevant issue is being ignored or overlooked then he or she will say so. In order for the programme to be effective, individuals will have to express opinions, and describe how they feel about the way a task was completed and how effectively they feel the group is operating. The more that individuals do this and the more honestly they do it, the more they will get out of the programme.

The trainer has his or her own opinions and ideas on what may or may not work for the inviduals or the group, and how they might operate most effectively, but they are just that. They should be listened to and seriously considered since he or she has a lot of experience working with groups, but if the participants feel that they do not fit, then they should be challenged. This can be a very productive process, as it often generates specific and very useful information about the group's or individual's work environment.

This is the information the group need to have. For this to be effective in generating the requisite environment and trust, it is absolutely crucial that the trainer behaves consistently and appropriately.

Guidelines for participants in the review process

The guidlines that are going to operate during the reviews constitute the next element to consider. These are often referred to as communication guidelines, and vary a lot from trainer to trainer and group to group. They are aimed at eliminating or forestalling some of the potential problems highlighted earlier. I normally split them into two subject areas: communication in review, and giving and receiving feedback. I also try to limit the number of guidelines in each section to three or four, since more than that is often too complex to be practical. Further, rather than impose them, I present and explain them to the group and than ask their agreement to using them, and their help in making sure that they are adhered to.

Those given below are the three most elegant and effective guidelines I have come across, and make up my preferred set.

1. I use 'I' rather than one, we, they, or you.

This asks each person to express opinions, perceptions, and emotions from his or her own individual point of view. This ensures that assumptions are not made about how other people experienced a particular aspect of a task, or how they feel about an issue or point of contention. Secondly, it ensures that when an opinion or piece of feedback is given it is owned by an individual, thus negating many of the techniques used by individuals (consciously or unconsciously) to manipulate other members of the group. Paradoxically when giving an opinion, or feedback, expressing it personally (using 'I'), adds emotional power and weight to it, making it more likely to be listened to and effective. This guideline also helps to eliminate the sort of confrontation for which there is often great potential in review, caused by inaccurate perceptions of how other people feel or 'should' feel, based on one's own beliefs, feelings and experience – in other words, not recognising that all individuals react uniquely to the world around them. When explaining and justifying this guideline to the group, I would normally use the points about how owning statements makes them more effective, and the need to avoid assumptions about how other people are reacting based on personal experience. I might also explain that they should avoid other general pronouns such as no-one and everyone.

2. I listen without interference, drifting, interrupting, or talking aside.

Drifting is a common phenomenon: whilst you are sitting listening to someone talk, your mind goes off at a tangent, triggered by the view out the window, or a phrase from the person speaking, so that effectively your body is present but your mind is a thousand miles away. Interruption can take many forms, and one is specified here: talking aside. This is the situation where, whilst an individual talks to the group as a whole, two members concurrently hold their own private (but usually obvious) conversation. The guideline focuses on two areas: firstly, it is asking the group members to respect each other, by listening to and considering each other's opinions; secondly, it helps the trainer to ensure that each group member has the chance to express an opinion without being interrupted or talked down. He simply phrases the question in such a way that each individual will be expected to reply. He then has an already justified and agreed way of preventing interruptions (if the group does not do it for him). One such question might be: 'I'd like you to think about the last task, and I'd like a comment from each of you about how successful you feel the group was in achieving the objectives. If you could start, John, and then we'll carry on around the room.'

3. I take full responsibility for my participation in this programme.

This relates back to the principle of individuals taking responsibility for themselves, in this instance in terms of how they feel, their own emotional welfare, and the consequences of their actions. In the context of a review it means that if an individual walks into a review feeling very strongly about something, but does not raise it, that individual is responsible for dealing with the subsequent stress or negativity he or she is likely to experience, as the rest of the group have no way of knowing what the issue is and hence how to deal with it. Conversely, if you raise a contentious issue in a review then you must not only raise it in a responsible manner, but also use your best efforts to resolve it. What is not acceptable is deliberately to raise a contentious issue and then to take no responsibility for trying to resolve it.

This third guideline effectively mitigates against people 'playing games' by making it obvious when they are doing so. If they do persist they can then be 'called', so lessening the impact of the issue, whatever it might be. This of course is the final and rather drastic response in terms of dealing with this particular issue, and in my experience it very rarely gets to this stage.

These then are to my mind the most effective guidelines I have come across for use within a review. They work on more than one level, are effective in dealing with the potential problems already outlined, and also help to make the reviews more focused and less time consuming.

Three other guidelines which I may occasionally introduce during reviews, or that are regularly suggested by groups are:

1. No put-downs.
This is self-explanatory and highlights a particular organisational culture that is sometimes encountered where one-liners and put-downs are used as a way of short-circuiting discussion and debate.

2. Get on, get off.
This is a very succinct way of expressing frustration with individuals who use constant repetition to reinforce a point. Again it is symptomatic of a particular organisational culture.

3. 'Calling'.
This is a concept I find useful when dealing with groups. There are a number of words or phrases likely to crop up during a review which cover a range of meanings, and are likely to mean different things to different people: communication, morale, team spirit, leader and so on. All of these have different meanings and connotations to different people, and some of these connotations have strong feelings attached. So I introduce the group to the idea of 'calling', as in the game of poker, when you want to find out what cards everyone else is holding. In the review this means 'calling' the individual who is using a certain word or phrase, by asking him or her to clarify exactly what is meant by it. For example, an individual might express a need to improve the group's communication; he could then be 'called' by another member of the group and asked to clarify exactly what aspect of communication he meant – listening skills, expression of ideas, building rapport, giving clear instructions, and so on.

Guidelines for giving and receiving feedback

Guidelines for giving feedback are much more common, although they are usually designed for the workplace rather than a review situation, where the dynamics are slightly different.

To be effective they need to tie in with, and follow on from, the review guidelines, and the ones I use in conjunction with the guidelines above are split into two areas: giving and receiving.

For the person *giving* the feedback there are two guidelines:

1. Describe specific behaviour, not character.
2. Describe the effect this behaviour has on you.

The first of these avoids the problems associated with labelling or categorising, instead describing behaviour, which of course can be modified. The second gives the person a specific, real reason why the person giving the feedback would like the behaviour to be changed (assuming the feedback is negative). For example, a bad piece of feedback would be:

> We all saw that you are bad at planning under pressure.

It makes a huge generalisation, is phrased in an unsympathetic and threatening manner, and labels the person as 'a bad planner', offering him or her little or no possibility of change.

In a review situation a more effective way for a participant to offer the feedback would be:

> When you had to alter the plan, you appeared to keep changing your mind, and be hesitating. Because of this I was no longer confident that the plan was workable, and hence I lost a lot of commitment and energy.

The person receiving the feedback knows exactly what the problematic behaviour was, and why it was causing difficulties for that individual. He or she also knows what to do to avoid a similar problem in the future: not to appear indecisive and hesitate when the pressure is on.

It is also a good idea to suggest guidelines for people receiving feedback, and these concern how a response should be made.

1. Only question for clarification.
2. Do not, under any circumstances, get into a conversation

starting: 'Yes, but . . .', or any other form of justification. (This is often seen as snubbing or discounting the individual and his or her feedback.)

3. The best response is always to listen carefully to the comments, ensure you have fully understood them, and finish by thanking the person for that feedback.

In a review situation, feedback is a very useful source of information both for the individual and the group, so these guidelines therefore aim to achieve three things. The first is accurate and usable information, which can be used to build a picture of how the group see each other, and which behaviours are and are not effective. The second is to provide an atmosphere in which feedback can be given easily, without stress for either the person giving or receiving it. The third is to encourage both individuals involved in the process to continue giving and receiving feedback in the future. The consequences of badly delivered feedback in a review are often difficult to deal with, both from the individual's and the trainer's point of view. It is therefore imperative that participants do follow the guidelines, whatever they may be, and the trainer monitors and coaches them in this process.

Confidentiality and reports

Confidentiality is one of the keys to building an environment which is open and supportive. For people to speak freely and without reserve it is important for them to feel that what they say will not be used against them at a later date. One of the benefits of using the outdoors, identified in an earlier chapter, was the opportunity to try out new ways of operating in a 'risk free' environment – in other words, where failure would not have any consequences in the workplace. For individuals to be confident of this, there needs to be an element of confidentiality, since otherwise potentially embarrassing failures could end up doing the rounds at work, with possible negative consequences for individuals.

There is however a potential conflict, as any organisation spending money on a training programme wants to be assured that they are getting value for money. Asking for reports is often seen as a way of checking on this, as well as providing additional information for any ongoing assessment or appraisal process. Aside from the obvious inherent difficulties of mixing assessment and training in the same programme, there are two problems: the inhibiting and distorting effect it is likely to have on people contributing fully to the reviews, and the whole question of how accurate the process would be.

The review process is aimed at generating useful information about the work environment, and for this to be successful, participants need to feel free to discuss not only the positive but the negative situations in their workplace. It is unlikely that any individual will do this freely, if they feel that whatever they say will be reported back to their organisation. By the end of the programme it is to be hoped that this situation will have been changed, since the aim of many programmes is to deal with negative workplace situations, but it will have taken time and skill on the part of the trainer to have developed the atmosphere in which this is possible, and the solutions will be generated and 'owned' by the participants themselves. In order for the trainer to be able to do this, it is vital that he or she can tell the participants that he will not be delivering any reports, and that anything said on the programme is confidential and will not be repeated back to the organisation without the specific agreement of the people concerned. This is particularly relevant in the situation mentioned earlier, where issues can be raised in review which cannot be resolved within the context of the programme; in this case the trainer's only option is to seek the group's approval to report this back to the client organisation, for them to deal with.

Using the outdoors as part of an assessment or appraisal process is a tempting idea, and is something that the armed forces have been doing successfully for many years. However it has always been recognised that this success stems from its forming part of a larger process, where conclusions or assessments are checked for congruence in a number of media. For example, a candidate appears to exhibit good planning skills when presented with a problem involving building a raft to cross a lake: how do those skills stand up when the candidate is asked to plan a social function on paper, or when questioned in detail about them in an interview? It may be that the candidate has previous experience of raft building. To be effective as an assessment tool, a programme would need to contain a number of other media, which would effectively swamp the main developmental aspects of a commercial programme.

The problems described above make it obvious that the group need to know where they stand at the beginning of the programme. For some of the more sophisticated groups no real guidelines are necessary, but for other, less sophisticated ones, the following two points usually suffice:

- Individuals' behaviour and performance should not be discussed with anyone who was not present on the programme.
- The trainer will not report on individuals to the client organisation, unless this has been made clear at the beginning of the programme; in which case the limitations of the course as an assessment tool will be stressed in the report.

As a final thought, if a report back is an essential part of the client's objectives, a good compromise is to structure the programme so that each individual produces a personal action plan, a copy of which is then given (with his or her permission) to the organisation. This gives the organisation a clear picture of the outcomes, without causing any of the problems highlighted above, and in addition can aid the support function which the organisation will need to provide if the programme is to be effective in the long term.

Personal and group outcomes

The relevance of personal outcomes is obvious in a programme aimed at personal development, where each individual is likely to have differing objectives; however, the relevance in other types of programme is perhaps less obvious and needs some explanation.

In the structure so far described, a great deal is asked of the participants with no apparent reward or gain for the individual, as so far it has all been focused on the client organisation. This is not a balanced or desirable state of affairs, since there is no real incentive, apart from loyalty and support for their organisation, for the individuals to take part and contribute fully. In the 'carrot and stick' motivation scenario, there is only the 'stick' of possible negative consequences in the workplace to induce the individuals to produce the effort, thought and commitment needed for a successful programme. Aside from the ethical considerations of using the 'stick', the mere possibility of its use is likely to negate any attempts to produce the open supportive environment needed to run a successful programme. What is required is a 'carrot', to persuade the participants to 'buy into' the programme, and motivate them to give it the effort and thought needed.

The most effective way to do this is to give each individual a personal stake in the end result, by asking each one to define exactly what outcomes he or she would like to gain personally from the programme. These outcomes should describe an issue, skill or achievement which the individual would like to make progress with, or attain, within the context of the programme. These personal outcomes can then be put into the same framework as the client's objectives (specificity, measurability, achievability, etc), and eventually, be incorporated into the transfer process. For those individuals for whom loyalty and support for the organisation is a motivating factor, it will reinforce and build on this – as it will on the organisation's objectives – since it is likely that these outcomes will support and reinforce them at a personal level. For those individuals for whom loyalty and support are not such motivational factors, it gives them a reason to take part fully, and make the programme a success, both for themselves and the organisation.

Group outcomes serve a slightly different purpose, and are useful when the programme objectives contain elements of teambuilding or team effectiveness. The team members are asked to set a number of outcomes that relate to how they would like the team to function, and/or what they would like the team to move forward on or achieve. This serves several useful functions:

- It starts to define the preferred style of operating for the group.
- It helps the bonding process between team members by producing mutually agreed outcomes, which they can then work together to achieve.
- It recognises and emphasises the unique 'character' of each team, further enhancing the bonding process.

- It provides the first step in the process by which the team takes responsibility for its own development.
- Because of the functions already listed, it enhances the commitment of the group to the programme.

As we have seen, the use of outcomes as part of a programme serves a number of functions; however their prime purpose (with the exception of personal development programmes) is to generate commitment to the review process, so that in turn they can generate the necessary information and feedback to make the programme a success.

Hidden agenda

It is likely that in any group attending a programme there will be individuals not fully committed to, and motivated by, the prospect. The issues involved might include:

- reservations about the outdoor – or indoor – elements of the programme
- reservations about the effectiveness of outdoor training in producing any real change
- pressure being applied on individuals to attend
- work issues
- reservations about the motives or commitment of the organisation's hierarchy to the process
- personal problems or issues which are distracting or disturbing the individual.

Whatever the reason, it is likely to be very real to the individual or individuals concerned, and, in order to move on and be able to contribute to the overall process, it is vital that they are given the opportunity to express them at the beginning of the programme. At least then they can be acknowledged, and possibly dealt with.

The importance of doing this cannot be overestimated. During a programme a trainer who does not at least recognise and acknowledge such an issue is like someone trying to hold a football under water with a clenched fist: no matter how hard he or she tries, it always pops up and hits him in the face; and the harder and further he pushes it below the surface, the faster and harder it comes back up again. In outdoor programmes this is especially true when the isues concern the parent organisation.

If people are given the chance to express such issues, and then agree to take responsibility for their participation in the pro- gramme, they can no longer treat the trainer as if he were a rep- resentative of the organisation. Instead, the issue 'belongs' to the individual, and the trainer's role becomes that of a coach or counsellor, helping that person to resolve it.

There are several techniques for carrying out this process, and one is described in more detail in an example programme in chapter 10 (page 148).

Cultural and gender issues

An outdoor programme provides a good medium to address issues relating to culture and gender, especially stereotyping. The type of tasks involved often bring these attitudes to the fore, where they are obvious to all, and the review provides an ideal forum in which their implications can be discussed and dealt with.

However, from experience it is pointless to press the issue unless the individual or individuals concerned express the desire to change that situation. On many occasions I have raised this issue, only to encounter the reply that they like things the way they are and there is no problem here.

If individuals do express such a desire, however faintly, then I feel that it is the trainer's role to support and encourage them as fully as is needed; but without that expressed wish, the trainer is wasting his or her time.

These then are the elements that go to make up the emotional 'safety net'. Taken together they form a complex system which is mutually supporting, and gives the trainer and participants the opportunity to express themselves freely and responsibly, in an open and supportive environment.

The final point to make in this chapter is a simple one. I have described a system that I know to be effective and simple to implement (see the example programme in chapter 10); however as with the basic assumptions described at the beginning of the chapter, this is not the only way of achieving the desired results.

By describing this system I hope I have highlighted the problems and issues that can arise during a programme. An alternative system can be used, but whatever its basis, it must address these problems and issues.

5

Task Design

The design of the tasks forms a major part of the programme structure. It is the tasks that generate information about behaviour and processes, without which the rest of the programme cannot function. In terms of producing a successful programme it is vital that the tasks reflect the issues and skills described in the objectives.

However this reflection or simulation is only part of the process; to be effective a task must satisfy three criteria:

Simulation is the mimicking of the situations which generate the issues, or require the skills, outlined in the programme's objectives.

Impact describes the effect that the task should have on the participants. It should engage their attention and interest, so that they become fully involved in the task and committed to achieving it. Furthermore, when the task is completed, the situations generated by the task should be memorable, so that when it is being reviewed the trainer can link specific learning to them, and these in turn can then be linked to work situations. This potentially creates an automatic process, whereby the work situation generates a memory of the task situation, which in turn generates a memory of the solution or learning associated with it.

Safety is of course a vital element in the task design process, and must never be ignored or underrated.

These then are the key elements involved in task design and in the remainder of this chapter they will each be discussed in more detail.

Simulation

Simulation is a delicate art; it is about creating an analogy of a work situation which requires certain skills or generates a specific issue, but which does not threaten the individuals or group concerned, so that they can operate naturally without any unusual stresses. To achieve this the simulation itself must not bear too close a superficial resemblance to the work situation, but on a deeper level must generate the same dynamics and relationships. One way of viewing this, as I have already suggested, is that by designing a task, you are generating a living parable in which the participants actually function and take part, and then review their own actions to decide what the moral was. Where this analogy breaks down is that you can only control the start of the process, and once it is handed over to the group, your ability to control or influence the end results is minimal. This is as it should be. One of the fundamental mistakes to make when designing tasks is to attempt to design the result, either making it impossibly hard, or very easy, in order to make specific points. Effectively this is manipulation of the group, and will be picked up by them very quickly. Whichever way you attempt to influence the result, it will be resented by the group, and will have a very negative effect on the review.

So the level of difficulty involved in a task is a key factor in the simulation process. As a very general guideline, I try to design the tasks so that the group is likely to be successful in about half of them. This is because I find that, on the whole, tasks where the groups only achieve a measure of success generate more useful information than those in which they are 100 per cent successful. Alternatively, if they are consistently unsuccessful, it tends to affect motivation and commitment to the programme, so that after a while the learning process again starts to suffer. If asked (and I always am), I declare this to the group, so that there are no illusions or issues about this sort of manipulation. As the programme progresses, the tasks are likely to increase in difficulty, to keep the group in the learning process and not resting on their laurels. Thus the group's normal perception of the tasks, as a series of tests which they must pass, is modified and they can begin to see them as tools for learning, whilst at the same time there is still an element of competition, with a standard against which they can measure themselves.

When designing the task, the first stage is to decide on the dynamics or interactions to be addressed, and then to prioritise them. This is where the flowchart of the issues or objectives comes into its own. The example given in the previous chapter (see pages 34–8) can now be used to identify the key skills and parameters that will define each of the tasks; the completed flow-chart is illustrated in the figure on page 63. These are then used as the basis from which the tasks are designed.

To illustrate this process I have attached a series of examples of tasks at the end of this chapter, each consisting of a copy of the brief the group would receive, a short description of how it is set up and run, and a description of the issues or skills it focuses on. *In the Kingdom . . .*, *Stepping Stones*, *Caving* and *Network* are all fairly standard tasks in general use with most outdoor providers; *Research* and *Soothsayer* are tasks I have designed in conjunction with clients to address specific objectives. It is normally the case when putting together a programme that the tasks will be a mixture of off-the-peg and purpose designed.

Tasks can be classified using a four-box model:

METHOD OF OPERATING

	KNOWN	UNKNOWN
OBJECTIVES KNOWN	1	3
OBJECTIVES UNKNOWN	2	4

A Type One task consists of a task with a defined and definite objective, and a clear, effective method of operating. The most

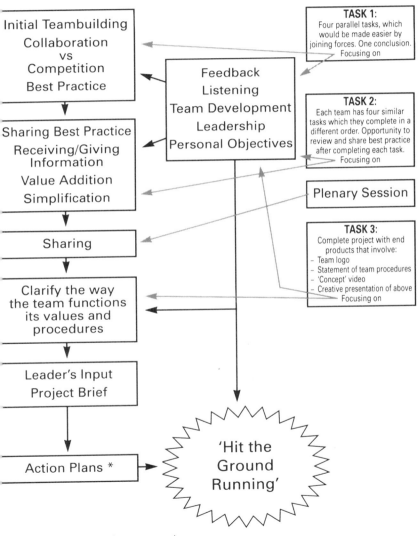

BP Teambuilding Event
28–30 June 1992
Issues/Task Flow Chart

Initial Teambuilding
Collaboration
vs
Competition
Best Practice

Sharing Best Practice
Receiving/Giving
Information
Value Addition
Simplification

Sharing

**Clarify the way
the team functions
its values and
procedures**

**Leader's Input
Project Brief**

Action Plans *

Feedback
Listening
Team Development
Leadership
Personal Objectives

TASK 1:
Four parallel tasks, which
would be made easier by
joining forces. One conclusion.
Focusing on

TASK 2:
Each team has four similar
tasks which they complete in a
different order. Opportunity to
review and share best practice
after completing each task.
Focusing on

Plenary Session

TASK 3:
Complete project with end
products that involve:
– Team logo
– Statement of team procedures
– 'Concept' video
– Creative presentation of above
Focusing on

'Hit the
Ground
Running'

* Covering team development and
project-related objectives

63

common type of work situation it is likely to simulate is a production, administration or information-handling process. The
most likely issues to arise in such a situation relate to dealing
with stress, and maintaining motivation, commitment and effective work processes, in an unstimulating and potentially monotonous environment. Not surprisingly, I have never been asked to
include such an exercise in a programme.

Type Two tasks consist of situations where the method of operating is clearly defined but the objectives are not. They can be
useful when looking at issues related to setting and achieving
goals, especially in a short task early in the programme. Again
their use is limited, because a significant aspect of an outdoor
programme is the provision of an interesting and stimulating
environment in which to learn, and more than one or two tasks of
this type would soon have a negative effect on this.

Tasks where the objective is clearly stated, but the means of
achieving it have to be devised by the group, are Type Three and
likely to form the majority of the tasks in the programme. These
seem to provide the best medium for focusing on the issues and
objectives usually set for outdoor programmes, whilst maintaining the level of stimulation necessary to maintain the interest and
commitment needed from the participants to make it successful.
Of course, they can be used to look at the areas of dealing with
stress and setting objectives, which are highlighted by Type One
and Two tasks.

Type Four tasks set problems where neither the objectives nor
the methods of achieving them are clear. This is the sort of problem that at work confronts middle and senior managers and it is
in programmes aimed at this level, or tasks focused on creativity,
that they tend to appear.

The dividing line between the different types of tasks is a little
artificial, since it would be easy to design a task that falls somewhere between Types Three and Four, or Two and Three, and so
on. However, I use it as a useful framework within which to
define the level and the purpose of the task.

Of the six tasks described at the end of this chapter and discussed below, five are Type Three and one is Type Four.

One of the most directly focused tasks I know of is *Stepping
Stones* (see pages 77–8). It is designed to look at simple (linear)

planning and organisational skills, and it is often used early in a programme to remind a group of, or introduce them to, some of the skills. In order to be successful the group need to carry out a number of functions:

- to have understood the brief and the implications of the restrictions
- to devise a method of bridging the gaps between the stones
- to plan the logistics of moving the whole team and equipment across the stones effectively, so that the equipment is always where it is needed, and there is no unnecessary or wasted movement of individuals
- to have carried out the previous two functions *before* starting to cross
- to implement and control the plan above
- to adapt the plan when they encounter the change in size of the gaps, halfway through the stones.

This is a simple but nonetheless effective task, since defects in planning and organisation are immediately (and often humorously) apparent. Reviewing can be direct and to the point.

A requirement in many programmes is a task to focus on communication within a team and how it affects success in the task, team members' attitudes, their motivation, and their personal involvement and commitment to the team's goals. *In the Kingdom . . .* (see pages 74–7) was designed specifically to look at these areas. For a team to succeed there is a need for specific, accurate, two-way communication between the communicator and other team members. The task highlights these areas on several levels.

- The first focus is the requirement for specific, directed and accurate instructions to each of the operators. This is the minimum essential for any success in the task.
- On the next level is the need to involve and inform the operators since they have not seen the equipment, the tokens they are recovering, or the equipment being used to recover it. In order to retain any motivation, most of them will need at least a description of the above and the opportunity to ask questions, and maybe to input ideas. It is the norm to find operators who

even after the task is finished are still not sure what they were doing, or why, or even the levels of success achieved.

- In the review this can then be developed into a discussion on individuals' differing needs in order to remain comfortable and motivated.
- The use of the supervisors can generate a number of issues, as there is a tendency to assume that their sole purpose is to guide the operators around the area. In reality, there are at least two other very useful roles open to them: identifying which containers contain tokens, and signalling fine adjustments in the 'hooking' process, since the communicator's ability to do this is severely limited by his or her fixed position.
- The way individuals each handle the issues generated for themselves is in itself a useful area to address. For example, if someone starts to attribute a lack of motivation to lack of information and involvement, it is very valid to ask that individual what he or she did to rectify the problem.

With its focus on the issues of communication, passage of information, involvement, two-way communication, and taking responsibility for one's own welfare, this is a particularly useful task in programmes aimed at graduates, supervisors and line managers in their intial appointments.

Caving (see pages 78–81) is often used in programmes, and the type of task varies enormously. Indeed, it is as much an activity as a task. I have described one particular approach because it illustrates the simulation process very effectively and is also one of the most effective ways to use caving in an outdoor programme.

Once the activity is set up as described, the purpose behind it and how it will be run must be explained; this sets the scene and gives the participants a framework within which to operate.

The activity is designed to focus on the processes of support and encouragement in a challenging environment; it also looks at individuals' levels of achievement, and the process of deciding at what point to say 'enough'. Finally, it is an activity that almost always generates a very positive experience of teamwork, with the consequent bonding effect.

The three activities described so far have been comparatively short and tightly focused on a particular area or interlinking set of issues. In these activities, the task design process focuses on three areas:

1. creating a situation where, in order for the group to achieve some level of success, they have to get involved in the areas of planning, communicating, encouraging, supporting, and so on
2. assessing the impact of their success or failure in carrying out these functions, and hence making it possible to draw conclusions, and, where appropriate, make modifications to improve or maintain these skills
3. making comparisons and connections to the workplace, in order to discuss and modify the conclusions and adaptations already made.

These tasks are fairly typical of the early part of a programme, but as a programme progresses there is usually a need to start increasing the level of difficulty and to provide a closer simulation of the workplace, so that, instead of focusing on one area or skill, there is a need for a range of skills (which previously have perhaps been addressed individually) to be used simultaneously and in support of one another.

The next three tasks are of this type. Each was designed to focus on a broad range of team and management skills, with in addition a dominant theme or focus for the task. In the case of the three given here these are respectively:

1. information gathering, organisation, and utilisation
2. negotiation skills in a complex and changing environment
3. creative thinking processes and devising specific effective strategies for the group.

All are much longer– lasting at least half a day – and generate a great deal of information about the group, which necessitates either an equivalent amount of time spent in review, or the trainer making choices about which areas the review will focus on.

The *Network* project (see pages 81–5) is a particularly effective project, as its structure seems to provide a clear goal on which participants can focus; the concept behind it is simple, and it requires the full spectrum of team and management skills, plus information handling, to be successful. It also raises the issue of co-operation and competition between teams, and so can be useful when dealing with sales teams. It is flexible and can be adapted to fit different groups and abilities, and it is particularly effective with real teams and with supervisors and line managers.

Research (see pages 85–9) is another complex project aimed at middle and senior managers, as it is designed to focus on negoti-ation skills and logical problem solving. Again in order to be successful, each group has to function at a high level, and as an effective team. Within that team there is then a requirement for various subgroups which need to be co-ordinated and managed.

Soothsayer (see pages 90–2) is a project focused on creativity and managing the creative process. It is a Type Four problem inasmuch as not only do the participants have to define a solu-tion, they must first define the problem, and in order to do this they must first learn to operate the information retrieval system.

The aim of this section has been to illustrate how the process of simulation can be achieved within the framework of a task or project. This of course is only the first element to be considered when designing tasks; the next element which needs to be looked at in conjunction with this is achieving impact.

Impact

This is where an outdoor programme justifies its existence. 'Impact' describes the way a particular task or project should grab the attention of the participants, so that they give it their undivided attention and become fully involved in it, and have a genuine interest in the outcomes. It also describes the process by which the task itself is designed to be memorable and stimulat-ing, so that learning associated with it is automatically 'keyed' whenever the task or similar situations are recalled. To give a simple example, abseiling is an activity often used as part of a task, to look at how people prepare for and deal with challenging situations. The process of gathering information, being trained in the skills, arriving on the site and deciding whether or not the task is within personal limits, gathering information from the first person to do it, being coaxed and encouraged by the remainder of the team, and finally the thrill or the relief felt on succeeding, or dealing with having decided not to do it, these are all extremely memorable experiences very unlikely to be forgotten. It is a relatively simple process to draw analogies and make connections between that set of experiences and similar issues that provide challenge for individuals in the workplace. Thus the next time that individual experiences a challenging situation in the workplace, he or she will have a set of very clear, strong memories of an analogous situation in which he or she was successful, and associated with those memories are the strategies needed to repeat that success. For those individuals who choose not to abseil, the review will illustrate how the process worked for others in the group, with their strategies. In addition, the trainer can use a later task and different activity to generate a personal positive experience of the process for them.

This is quite a strong example and most programmes are unlikely to involve more than one or two exercises as overtly challenging as this. There are a number of ways of achieving impact within a task, of which the sort of physical challenge described above is only one. Some of the others are:

Novelty: trying out new skills, solving problems in different mediums, experiencing new and unfamiliar environments.

Excitement: doing things that are perceived as exciting, or having the opportunity to get involved in things that would otherwise not be readily available.

Enjoyment: providing activities that the participants can enjoy whilst taking part in the programme. For many people just working outside can be a very enjoyable process.

Humour: using an element of the ridiculous (in moderation) can often help to generate interest.

Mental challenge: exercising the imagination and intellect with problems never previously encountered, so giving the freedom to devise new and innovative solutions.

Competitiveness: making use of the desire to perform better than others or oneself in a different medium. (This should be used cautiously otherwise it can often get in the way of the remainder of the programme.)

The caving activity described at the end of the chapter is so effective because it combines all the elements listed above, with a direct, clear focus on the issues involved. On a personal level, I first went into a cave 14 years ago as part of a process of personal development, and can still picture many of the experiences and remember the feelings generated by the trip extremely clearly, even today.

The *Stepping Stones* task (see pages 77–8) is effective because it presents an apparently simple task which soon proves to be complex and much more subtle than expected, providing an element of mental challenge as well as generating novel and slightly ridiculous situations.

In the Kingdom . . . (see pages 74–7) involves elements of novelty, mental challenge and competitiveness.

The three projects are rather more complex. Each contains sub-tasks which use the methods listed above as ways of generating involvement, but in addition there is a further element that operates with respect to the overall project. In each case, aside from the factors listed above, there is an element of involvement, and each has its own complex structure with a range of possible actions, consequences, options and measures of success: effectively a complex, involving and very realistic game, with real consequences, rather like an enhanced virtual-reality video game with real consequences. Well-designed projects generate an involvement and commitment from the participants which on occasions I find hard to credit, and can only account for by referring to the sort of game and role-playing they allow.

To summarise, impact is a crucial part of task design, and can be achieved in a variety of ways. The outdoors has a major advantage over other media, not only because of the huge variety of choices it offers, but for the vast majority of the working population it is an unknown and/or only partially explored world. Hence the opportunities to experience new, exciting and stimulating situations are huge, with limits imposed only by cost, safety and the imagination.

Safety

We have already discussed on a number of occasions the issue of safety. Technical safety, for example the running of a climbing task, a construction task (bridging a gorge), or a task like *In the Kingdom . . .* is a very specialised field, requiring both expertise and experience, and the chapter on resourcing programmes will discuss how to assess competence in this area.

The 'physical safety net' was another major element which helped make up the structure of the programme. Part of the 'net' involved task design, not only in terms of technical safety (for which you are likely to need competent assistance), but in terms of giving individuals choice as to what role they take, and the level of challenge to which they subject themselves. We are looking to give people experiences to stretch their limits, and, if they wish to push themselves that hard, a 'frontier experience'. What is not acceptable is to allow them to get into the 'panic zone', as illustrated in the figure on page 3.

To re-emphasise a point already made, one individual's 'frontier experience' may well barely move out of another's comfort zone; equally, different elements of a task will challenge individual members of the team to differing degrees.

The case for a range of roles within each task is clear, so let us now look at how this is achieved, by taking the example given above of abseiling. The activity can be used as part of a larger task – one I have often run involves organising a search and recovery operation in a large area of ground below a disused road bridge, recovering the objects to the top of the bridge and assembling them correctly, with the only access to the ground being a descent from the bridge by means of a 25 metre abseil. There are various restrictions on how many descents and ascents each individual may make, the number of objects each may recover, and so on. The task is designed for a group of about eight, and there are a number of viable roles: searching for the objects (requiring a descent by abseil), operating the safety equipment (monitored by an instructor), co-ordinating the individual search areas (best done from the top of the bridge), keeping track of descents and recoveries, and assembly of the finished item on the bridge. All these need to be carried out and it is up to the group how they organise themselves to do this; they can swap roles so that everyone has a chance to abseil, or they can cater for an individual or individuals who do not wish to abseil, by giving them other, specific roles. It is very much the team's task to make these allowances (as in the workplace), and the instructor will only step in if he or she feels that this is not being done and people are likely to suffer as a consequence. (If it is necessary to step in it is useful for the trainer if the instructor tells the group very clearly at the time exactly why he feels it necessary to intervene.) In this task I have occasionally come across the situation where one individual in the group is prepared to abseil but not to operate the safety equipment and take responsibility for another's safety, and another who is happy to operate the safety equipment but for whom abseiling is out of the question.

In the other tasks described the variation of roles should be clear. In *In the Kingdom* . . . the roles are clearly defined for the group as part of the exercise brief. The *Stepping Stones* task is not normally considered to be physically challenging; however, it provides a number of process roles: planner, scout, manager, timekeeper and progress monitor, and so on.

The caving activity achieves the same end but by different means. Here the group is briefed that each individual will make his or her own decision about the level of challenge they wish to set, and that each can make his or her own decision about when to stop the exercise. In addition, there is still the variation of roles available within the group, and they are very real with serious responsibilities: providing information support and encouragement to other members of the group, exploring and reporting back to the group, monitoring individuals' 'state of mind', decision making and so on.

The projects provide a wider range of roles, ranging from managing the overall process, through problem solving and analysis, leading smaller tasks (with all the roles involved in them), gathering and collating information, to supporting, informing and encouraging other team members, and many more.

So far we have talked about two factors to take into account when designing tasks. There is a third, which whilst obvious must be stated: the level of physical fitness and agility needed to undertake and successfully complete the task must be appropriate to the group. Thus a task that involves collecting information on foot from a variety of locations must be matched, and if need be modified, during the programme to fit the abilities of the group. This is potentially the most likely cause of injury or accident within a programme and must be carefully monitored throughout.

To summarise, there are three factors to focus on in respect of safety when designing tasks:

1. technical safety, the nuts and bolts of running safe tasks, which range from abseiling and caving through construction type tasks to *In the Kingdom . . .* and *Stepping Stones*
2. variety or flexibility in the available roles, so that all participants can take up a role that will stretch them, but will not push them beyond their individual limits
3. matching the fitness and agility required to complete the tasks successfully to the particular group undertaking them.

These then are the three areas involved in designing effective outdoor tasks: simulation of the processes or issues involved in the course objectives; impact, providing a memorable experience that relates directly to the issues involved; providing a safe environment in which this can happen.

For a competent trainer, specialist knowledge or input will only be needed to a certain extent when looking at creating impact, and an outdoor specialist will be able to advise and give ideas on this from a much more detailed and expansive knowledge of the medium.

More importantly, however, is the question of safety, and this is where specialist knowledge is imperative, particularly when looking at the 'nuts and bolts' and the matching of abilities. The ability to do this comes through experience and expertise, practised over a number of years, and it is not something that can be learned from a book – indeed, much of it is not written down at all. So, unless you already possess these skills, and up to the required level, they need to be brought in. (How to assess the level of skills required is discussed in the chapter on resourcing.) Even running a comparatively simple task involving barrels and planks or *Stepping Stones* requires experience; indeed, although I do not have any statistics to hand, my feeling is that these types of tasks are more likely to generate accidents than those apparently more dangerous activities such as abseiling or climbing. Of course, one area in which the trainer can have significant input without specialist help is in the provision of different roles.

So if you wish to design your own outdoor tasks or projects, go ahead, but you will need to consult a specialist to ensure that they are safe, and perhaps to help enhance their impact.

Examples of outdoor tasks and projects

This section consists of a series of examples of outdoor tasks and projects. Three are short specific tasks, focusing on specific areas, and three are longer and much more involved, and hence are referred to as projects. Each example starts with a copy of the written brief given to the group, or a description of the verbal brief they receive prior to the task, and there then follows a short description of how the exercise is set up and how it is designed to run. Some of them could be adopted within organisations solely on the basis of the instructions given; others are included to give a flavour of the range of options in outdoor training.

In the Kingdom . . . is set up as shown opposite; the brief appears on page 76. A token is placed inside about one in three of the containers, which are opaque. Fifteen of them are placed randomly in a circle about two metres in diameter, in the centre of the restricted area, which itself needs to be at least six metres in diameter, and (within reason) the larger the better.

The apparatus to retrieve the containers and the tokens inside them needs to be suspended on a rope above the restricted area; this rope needs to run across the centre of the area at least two metres off the ground, but with sufficient slack in it such that at the centre of the restricted area it is no more than one metre off the ground.

74

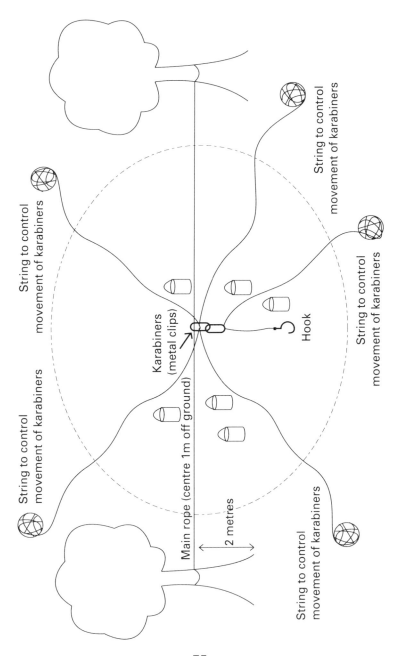

String to control movement of karabiners

String to control movement of karabiners

String to control movement of karabiners

String to control movement of karabiners

String to control movement of karabiners

String to control movement of karabiners

Karabiners (metal clips)

Hook

Main rope (centre 1m off ground)

2 metres

In the Kingdom...

Your task is to recover as many tokens (indicated by the Trainer) as you can from a restricted area in 30 minutes.

There are various restrictions on the team:

❑ Before moving to the area you must allocate three roles:

- ○ **Blind Operators** (minimum two, maximum five)
- ○ **Mute Supervisors**
- ○ **Communicators**

❑ Operators must be blindfolded before they can approach the task site and throughout the task. Roles may not be changed during the task.

❑ Only Operators may work the recovery equipment; no-one else may touch any part of the equipment or items.

❑ The equipment cannot be reconfigured/changed or adapted.

❑ Only Supervisors may go inside the restricted area. They must remain mute throughout the task.

❑ Communicators must remain at the locations indicated by the Trainer throughout the task.

Once the items have been collected on the recovery equipment, they can be collected in the box held by the Mute Supervisor.

...of the Blind

This then allows the group to manoeuvre the recovery equipment over any of the containers. The recovery equipment itself consists of a hook attached to some cord which runs through a karabiner, and this karabiner itself is attached to another karabiner which can move freely along the rope. Thus the whole system can be guided over any of the containers by pulling on cords attached to the top karabiner. The hook can then be lowered to hook the container's handle, and the whole system moved to one end of the rope where an operator can then recover it and (hopefully) the token. The tokens are golf balls with the word TOKEN written prominently on them, and the containers sprayed tin cans with upright wire handles attached.

The way in which the exercise is run can drastically affect the results and information generated for the review. The exercise as described is set up for six to nine people.

The participants are not allowed to see the apparatus before the task, and are given no information about it. They are given the brief, and asked to nominate roles; the operators are blindfolded and then taken with the remainder to the site, where once in view all the restrictions of the task are imposed. Chairs are placed on the edge of the restricted area on which the communicator/s must sit and remain throughout the exercise (see also page 66). Once the task is completed the operators must keep their blindfolds on until they are back in the review room (out of sight of the task), and the exercise must not be discussed among the group until they are in the review room. This serves to maintain any strong emotions or feelings among individuals (for instance, the operators often want to know what has been going on) so that they can be expressed and discussed in the review.

As already stated, success in this task involves clear precise communication, co-operation between all three roles, and hence maintenance of motivation and commitment for all three. It can be frustrating, and success seems to happen exponentially, perhaps because of the learning process; so it might take 15 minutes to recover the first container (with or without a token), 10 minutes the next, and the next two or three in the remaining five minutes. A group that is poor in communication skills might recover only one in the whole time, or even fail altogether.

Stepping Stones is set up as shown overleaf. The critical factor is the accurate distance between the 'stones', which ideally consist of two breeze blocks laid together to form a square. The equipment provided consists of two two-metre planks, capable of supporting the heaviest member of the team, and about two metres of light cord. The distances for setting up are given in the diagram.

To run the exercise, the group are brought to the task site, given the brief (overleaf), told how much time they have for the task (usually about 30 minutes), and then told to begin. In the early stages of a programme it is quite possible that a group will either leap in without any planning, and complicate the task further, or indulge in what a colleague of my mine labels as a spot of 'analysis/paralysis' for an excessive amount of time, before suddenly remembering the time constraints and charging into the task pell-mell.

The *caving* activity as described here does not have such a rigid format, with defined parameters of success and failure; it is

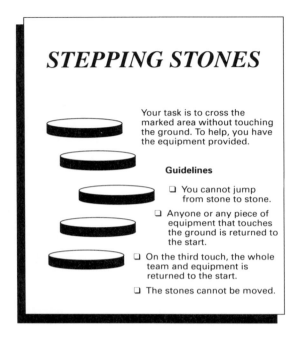

STEPPING STONES

Your task is to cross the marked area without touching the ground. To help, you have the equipment provided.

Guidelines

❏ You cannot jump from stone to stone.

❏ Anyone or any piece of equipment that touches the ground is returned to the start.

❏ On the third touch, the whole team and equipment is returned to the start.

❏ The stones cannot be moved.

presented to the participants as a learning experience rather than a task, and for this reason is often best located in the middle of a programme rather than at the start.

To a much greater extent than abseiling or climbing, every caving site is different both in its layout and the objective hazards it presents, so that caving tasks are designed for specific sites, and are usually unworkable and dangerous if attempted on a different site. (The implications in terms of finding qualified/experienced instructors is discussed in the chapter on resourcing.) This particular task is designed for a caving system much used by a variety of groups in South Wales called Porth yr Ogof. The cave itself is a complex system, with a river running through it, and can be divided into three areas: the dry series, the wet series and the exit. The activity takes place in the dry and wet series.* The

* The exit is extremely dangerous unless you know exactly what you are doing, are properly equipped, and know the cave well. There have been several deaths there over the years. In my opinion there is no justification, and indeed no need, to take groups involved in a commercial training programme into this area, although this opinion is not necessarily shared by all outdoor providers operating in the area.

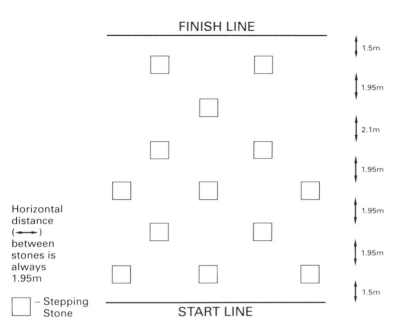

FINISH LINE

1.5m

1.95m

2.1m

1.95m

Horizontal
distance
(◄──►)
between
stones is
always
1.95m

1.95m

1.95m

☐ – Stepping
    Stone

START LINE

1.5m

cave can simplistically be described as funnel shaped, with a very large main entrance (20 metres by six metres), and as you progress further into the system the passages narrow and the obstacles become more difficult.

The task is introduced to the participants with a verbal briefing, which would run as described below.

When the participants have been informed that caving is next on the agenda, the first thing to do is address their concerns about this activity, and this is best done by an instructor.

He or she lists on a flipchart the aspects of caving that cause the group concern; they would normally produce a list that included:

- water – getting wet, or falling into deep water
- confined spaces – getting stuck, claustrophobia and so on
- roof falls and cave-ins
- wildlife – bats, rats and spiders
- cold

and various others . . .

This is then used as a framework around which the instructor can base a factual description of the cave system, which can then allay (or occasionally confirm) those concerns; certainly those listed above would all be allayed. At the end of this process the group then have a clear factual description of the cave environment, with special attention paid to their worries or concerns.

So far the view has been rather negative, so the next stage is to get the group to produce positive reasons for wanting to go into the cave; again these are listed, and the instructor checks that each individual has something that he or she can relate to on this list. Only then would the trainer step in and explain what the purpose of the activity was, and how it would work. This is done by describing the role the instructor will take in the exercise, making the following points:

- To start with he or she will lead the group, explaining the environment to them, showing them how to move underground and negotiate simple obstacles, and offering support and encouragement.
- As the trip progresses this role will change, and he or she will start to offer them options and choices about which passages to take by describing what each entails; at the same time members of the group can start to take the lead in negotiating obstacles and passages, and reporting back to the rest of the group on how difficult or easy they are, and so on.
- By the end of the trip the instructor will be relegated to the post of technical and safety advisor, offering more challenging options, with the group making decisions about which to take, organising themselves to meet them, and providing support and encouragement to individuals who need it.
- For the group it is an exercise that focuses directly on encouragement and support.
- For the individual it is the opportunity to experience a totally new and unusual environment, to practise encouragement and support skills, and to stretch personal limits in what may be a challenging environment; indeed if the participants are going to get any benefit from the exercise they must endeavour to do this.
- Finally, it is possible that at some point in the trip individuals are going to reach their limits and exercise their right to stop;

part of the function of support means ensuring that the group respect that decision and that the individual concerned experiences no negative consequences as a result of it.

This then is the way the activity is structured, and in reality the instructor plays a coaching role for a large part of the task, helping the group develop effective strategies and matching the level of challenges offered, to the level the group are at, at each point in the exercise. This requires both a detailed knowledge of the cave system and a great deal of experience of managing groups.

In terms of modelling support and encouragement skills within a group this exercise is very successful. It also provides a very effective 'bonding' experience for real teams.

The *Network Project* as described in the brief (see page 82) is designed for three teams of about eight members, each operating from similar briefs. Included with each brief are maps of the area, and six clues to start them on the network.

The network diagram (see page 83) is the heart of the project. Each point represents an actual location within three kilometres of the venue, where the details of a problem can be collected. Once solved this then generates the information that leads to subsequent points. As the network diagram implies, points 1 and 2 each provide information which when combined leads to point 7 and so on.

The problems vary according to the course objectives and the abilities of the group, but would usually involve a mixture of tasks similar to those already described, research problems, codes and ciphers, brain teasers, photographs of locations, and tapes in foreign languages. In the case of this particular project the final task, described at point 17, involved building a raft and using it to recover several bottles of champagne from the bottom of a rapid in the middle of the river Wye.

One of the areas that the project focuses on is the issue of competition versus co-operation between teams from the same organisation, a perennial problem especially in sales focused organisations. As the project progresses the teams begin to realise that the locations are the same for each team, and further into the task it becomes apparent that there is one box at site 17, with three different combination locks on it. The final task

NETWORK PROJECT

Your task is to gain access to the locked metal box at Site 17 and carry out the final challenge which is explained inside.

To gain access to the box, you will need to know the numbers of a four-figure combination. The numbers can be found at Sites 7, 9, 11 and 15. The order in which they fall in the combination can be found at Sites 8, 6, 13 and 16.

To help you identify and locate the whereabouts of each site, there is a system of colour coded circles and quadrants. The system is fully explained at Site 13.

The sites are further divided into 3 categories:

> Those within a 1km radius of the hotel
> Those within a 2km radius of the hotel
> Those within a 3km radius of the hotel

As you progress through the network you will incur costs. They are as follows:

> Organisational costs
> Travel expenses
> Fees and fines

These costs can be met by gaining income from each site that you visit. The amount available at each site is shown on the attached sheet. You have a £200.00 initial loan.

The financial requirements of the exercise are as follows:

> i) That you must produce a detailed account at the end of the exercise.
> ii) That you should remain in credit.
> iii) That you are in a position at the end of the exercise to repay your £200.00 loan.

Organisational Costs
Costs of £100.00 are due one hour after the commencement of the exercise and every hour thereafter.

Travel
You have four methods of travel:

> By foot
> By bicycle
> By taxi
> By ferry.

Travel by foot is free.

Bicycles
You have two bicycles available to you each at a cost of £5.00 per 15 mins (or part of), that they are being used. They must be checked out and back in at control. Failure to check them back in will incur continual hire charges.

However, before you may hire the bicycles you must first produce one bicycle token for each bicycle you wish to hire. The tokens are located at sites 5 and 6 and are within a 1km radius of the hotel.

Taxis
There is an exercise taxi company based at the hotel. They only have two cars available between all the teams. They work on a first come, first served basis. The charges are: £1.00 per minute that they are away from the hotel and £2.00 per mile. Surprisingly they have no local knowledge and therefore must be directed precisely.

Ferry
There is also a ferry which crosses the River Wye from in front of the Saracen's Head public house. The fee is 50p per person (real money).

People may not operate away from the hotel on their own. A minimum of pairs is required for all forms of travel.

Sites 12 and 14 are problem-solving exercises within the hotel grounds. You may only undertake them on production of the required notification and fee. The tasks are in sealed envelopes and you will not know the task until you have chosen one. All tasks have a time limit of 25 minutes. Failure to complete the task will halt progress via that route.

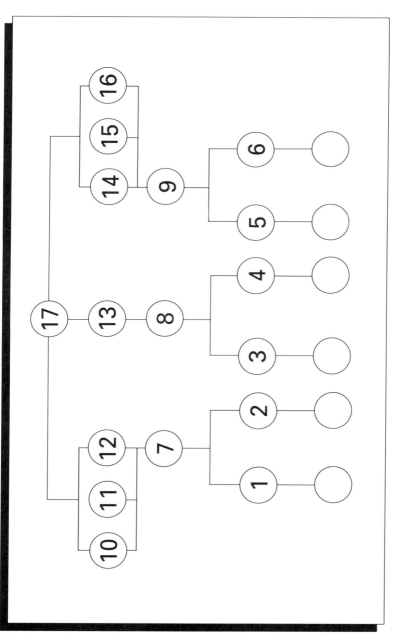

SITE	INCOME
1	£75.00
2	£75.00
3	£75.00
4	£75.00
5	£75.00
6	£75.00
7	£50.00
8	£50.00
9	£50.00
10	£75.00
11	£50.00
12	£25.00
13	£200.00
14	£25.00
15	£50.00
16	£75.00
17	**LOCKED BOX**
18	**FINAL CHALLENGE**

requires the combined resources and manpower of all three teams. One of the issues that is well worth exploring in the subsequent review is at what stage the groups decide to co-operate and why, how willingly did they do this, to what level, and what obstacles they had to overcome to do this.

The other areas that it particularly focuses on are: co-ordinating a number of different subgroups working on different tasks, organisation and collation of data, passage of information, and maintaining commitment and motivation in a changing or fluid situation.

The version given here was designed for a graduate programme, and typically would last about eight hours.

Research is a typical management task, whose (deliberately) obscure instructions often require a joint effort to decipher. It focuses on effective negotiation, financial management, team skills, and the communication and motivation issues that arise in a team carrying out a number of closely interdependent functions.

It is designed for a number of teams of up to 10 participants. The concept behind it is simple. Each team has a specific problem to solve, the problems are similar in nature, but have different solutions. Solving the problems requires resources (man-hours), and these can only be earned by completing tasks. Each team has a number of tasks available to it, and a number of resources; unfortunately the tasks and resources do not match. Simply pooling resources is not a strategy that will work. So, in order to complete the tasks, each team needs to negotiate with the other teams to obtain what it needs. The project is complex and each will have to negotiate several times before they successfully complete it.

Again the level and the difficulty of the project can be varied to fit the client, the version given here being aimed at junior and middle managers.

TELEX: STATION ZAW – DTG: 0900LOCAL

AFTER A RECENT TAKEOVER YOUR COMPANY HAS FOUND ITSELF THE OWNER OF A LARGE PHARMACEUTICAL COMPANY.

IN THE SUBSEQUENT REORGANISATION YOUR TEAM HAS BEEN DRAFTED IN TO REPLACE A RESEARCH GROUP THAT RESIGNED EN MASSE AFTER THE TAKEOVER.

YOUR OBJECTIVE IS TO COMPLETE THEIR TASK (AS OUTLINED IN THE ATTACHED PROJECT UPDATE) BY DELIVERING A CONFIRMED RESULT TO THE OPERATIONS DEPARTMENT. THIS MUST BE DONE WITHIN THE ORIGINAL TIME-SCALE PREDICTED AND WITHIN BUDGET.

THE ONLY TECHNICAL INFORMATION YOU HAVE AVAILABLE TO YOU IS CONTAINED IN THE RECENT PROJECT REPORT ATTACHED (ANNEXE A).

ALL OTHER INFORMATION ATTACHED IS CORRECT AS OF 0850HRS TODAY.

SEVERAL OTHER TEAMS FROM YOUR COMPANY ARE IN SIMILAR SITUATIONS.

ALL THE RELEVANT DOCUMENTS ARE ATTACHED.

RESEARCH PROJECT UPDATE
Alpha Pharmaceuticals Research Dept. 032

Our current priority is decoding the formula for TOADOFF, a chemical that acts as an environmentally friendly toad-repellent that can be used on highways, thus helping preserve an endangered species. So far this project has aroused a lot of interest in conservation and horticultural circles and generated a lot of much-needed positive PR. Unfortunately it is proving quite a time-consuming task to carry out and our budget for man-hours is nearly depleted.

A detailed description of our progress is attached at Annexe A, but briefly we now have a working example of the molecule and a notation (8 space grid) for describing its structure. The operations team are happy that once we give them the correct structure notation, production can start immediately. We still have to determine this, and this is the current problem area: the process for analysing consists of shooting rays into the grid and analysing the results; this is carried out for us by an outside contractor with whom the company has given us a budget of man-hours; the process is not time consuming but is very people intensive. Our current deadline for presenting a completed grid to Operations is 6.30pm on 2 July 1991.

A statement of the current man-hours situation is attached at Annexe B. **(Annexe B has been updated to represent the correct figure for today.)**

Our options at the moment are twofold:

> Apply for an increase in the man-hours allocated to us.
> Attempt to earn extra man-hours.

A paper has already been submitted to the Board with regard to the first option; in the unlikely event (considering the potential of the product) of this not being granted* some comments on the feasibility of earning extra man-hours are given below, and in more detail in Annexe C.

We have various tasks in hand which, whilst not directly relevant, could be used to earn extra man-hours:

> Satellite.
> Tokyo Rose.
> Great Escape.
> Egypt.
> Submersible.

In addition we have various resources and skills which could be used to earn further man-hours:

> Manpower.
> Karabiners.
> Ropes.
> Language skills.

* Extra man-hours have not been granted.

ANNEXE A

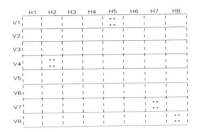

Shown above is an example of the Grid developed to describe the structure of the molecule/chemical; in this case it represents a simple plastic polymer. The information passed to operations will consist of 4 references regarding the positions of individual atoms (ie for this molecule H2, V4; H5, V1; H7, V7; H8, V8). To obtain this information the contractors have set up an electron microscope with a sample of the substance. When requested they fire a beam of electrons along a specific axis (vertical or horizontal) and pass back information as to what has happened to it. We can then interpret this using the experimental data on beam behaviour we have already acquired.

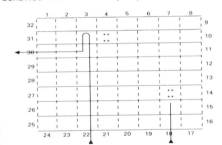

SOME EXAMPLES
OF BEAM BEHAVIOUR:

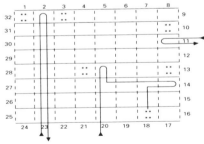

Beams exhibit two patterns of behaviour when they are shot along the numbered channels: they are either absorbed or deflected as shown, and sometimes they are affected by more than one point. The contractors can establish one of two things: either that the beam has been absorbed, or its exit point.

We are confident that it is now only a matter of time (and man-hours) to write the grid structure and reap immense benefits and profits from this project.

ANNEXE B

MAN-HOURS REPORT

Of the initial budget of some 9,000 man-hours of research time allocated to this project, some 750 remain.

The expenditure was as follows:

> 4,750 Research. (Contractor costs.)
> 2,000 Administration.
> 1,100 Conferences.
> 400 Sickness.

Contractor costs currently are as follows:

Each beam firing:	60 man-hours
Confirmation/denial of location of an individual atom:	100 man-hours
Confirmation/denial of location of all 4 atoms:	200 man-hours

ANNEXE C

Attached are more detailed descriptions for the potential tasks mentioned in the main brief and also for the skills and resources mentioned. If this option is selected there are various factors to be aware of:

Each task may only be attempted once.

Prior agreement of the contractor must be gained before starting any task; this will take about 40 minutes, and it will usually (but not always) be forthcoming.

Each member of the group must take part in at least 2 tasks.

The man-hours earned per task do not take into account the company profit generation scheme (see Annexe D).

Union and copyright restrictions are detailed in the descriptions where relevant.

It is possible to purchase or hire skills, resources and tasks from other groups, but all such transactions must be registered with the contractor, otherwise they are not valid.

In the past the contractor has always proved amenable to negotiation, and on occasions has even given credit.

Between the three groups the following resources are available:

Manpower	Knot-tying
Transport	Karabiners
Rope	Language skills
Maps	Video equipment
Photocopying	Compasses

A resource list for the tasks is at Annexe E.

ANNEXE D

COMPANY PROFIT GENERATION SCHEME

In accordance with the guidelines laid down by the Bankers a profit generation scheme has been set up whereby more resources are allocated to successful departments, success being judged by the number of tasks completed.

Thus for each task completed the department is rewarded with 10% more than the task reward, and this goes up by 10% for each successive task.

ie 1st success 10%, 2nd success 20%, 3rd success 30% etc.

In order to encourage diversification a profit bonus is also paid for each new area from which tasks are attempted. This is a straight bonus of 500 man-hours, paid to each group whenever tasks from a new area are successfully completed by one of the groups. The task areas are:

1. Video, Satellite.
2. Tokyo Rose, Operation Shylock, Chemical Waste Disposal, & Great Escape.
3. SRT, Submersible, & Blind Climbing.
4. Safecracker, The Electric Fence, & Skyhook.
5. Dark Room, Giraffe, & Sphinx.

ANNEXE E

RESOURCE LIST

Listed below are *some* of the resources that you will need to carry out the tasks.

Chemical waste recovery – Transport, map, compasses.
SRT – Transport, map, karabiners, ropes.
Electric Fence – Ropes.
Sphinx – ?
Satellite – video eqpt.
Tokyo Rose – Transport, compass, map.
Great Escape – ?
Grotto – ?
Submersible – Ropes?
Video – video eqpt.
Operation Shylock – Map, compass.
Blind Climbing – Transport, map, karabiners, ropes.
Safecracker – Rope?
Skyhook – Ropes.
Giraffe – ?

SOOTHSAYER

Your only source for clarification, assistance and information in this project is the Soothsayer, an archaic but effective information retrieval system.

Your access to the system is limited, and you only have basic instructions for operating it. You will have to experiment to learn the subtleties of the system.

You have until 4pm to complete the project.

SOOTHSAYER OPERATING INSTRUCTIONS

Information and assistance is generated by drawing lines and creating new points on the screen during your access time. Your access time is signified by a small BLUE square showing on the bottom left hand corner of the screen.

1. You may only draw one line and create one point during each access period.
2. Each line must start and finish at a point.
3. Each line must start at, finish at, or intersect an existing point twice, and a newly created one once.
4. No more than three lines may connect at any point.
5. No line may cross itself or any other line.

Soothsayer will only produce information when all these criteria are fulfilled.

Your current financial state is given in the top LEFT hand corner of the screen.

You may only enter the area around the screen during your team's access time.

Soothsayer is a Type Four problem, aimed at senior managers, with a focus on creativity and managing the creative processes of teams operating in a complex and changing environment.

The task is one of the most complex ones that I know of (and so can appear somewhat mystifying), in that it involves designing and creating or manufacturing a product, usually one that is relevant to the group. Since it is a Type Four problem, it also involves discovering and then defining what the product is, further refining the criteria for it, and then determining how to create/manufacture it. The project can be run with up to five teams of five to nine participants.

The physical focus of the task is a large whiteboard (2 metres square), divided into a number of different areas and with a number of points already marked on it. Learning to use the screen by the apparently complex rules given generates a broad range of information. As groups become more proficient, they can start to generate information on specific subjects, typically the definition of the overall task, creative techniques and processes, options for manufacturing, methods of earning and further information (including financial) on operating the screen. Each area of the whiteboard generates information on one of these subjects. In addition, there is a moderately complex financial structure to get to grips with as the task unfolds, which involves earning money to pay operating costs by carrying out smaller tasks throughout the project.

At the start of the project, the board might look like this:

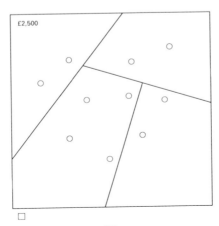

After a number of moves, the board might look like this:

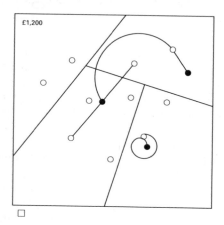

Each new point created (●) costs the group financially.
Each new connection generates information.
Possible connections are:

6

Review Design

Reviewing is for the trainer the key skill, and review and review skills form a critical element of the programme. We have already discussed the role of the trainer, and his or her relationship with the group. This chapter really concerns itself with one thing: describing how a trainer is able to focus the review on the relevant issues. This ability to run focused reviews is paramount to the success of a programme.

Most proficient outdoor trainers do not consciously sit down and design and structure a review as described here, as successful structures, verbal patterns and techniques have been assimilated on a subconscious level. However in order to do this, they had first to function and learn on a conscious level, and this is the process described here. You will see in the sample programme (chapter 10) a set of review guidelines; these are not meant to dictate methods of operating, but to ensure that there is congruence and compatibility in terms of style, issues raised and theories and models used, between trainers working on the same programme.

We have already (in chapter 4) described the role of the trainer, and its implication in terms of the attitudes and approach to the review process. We have also seen how flowcharting the issues or objectives of a programme starts to define the focus and parameters of the tasks, and this in turn defines the likely area to be examined or addressed by the review of that task.

An important point to make in relation to this is the importance of having flexibility or latitude in the review element of the programme. At the start of the programme the format or the design of the review for each task will have been discussed and specified. In doing this the trainers are attempting to predict the issues that each task will raise, a task in which they are unlikely to be 100 per cent accurate. There is a strong possibility that as a result of one of the tasks or the reviews, an unexpected issue is going to raise its head at some point during the programme. It is therefore a key and as yet unmentioned quality of trainers on outdoor programmes that they be flexible, and when they encounter such a situation able to think on their feet, either changing the review to deal with the new issue, or resolving it in some other way that is not going to cause problems later on.

The need for design in the review process is dictated by the inherent potential in outdoor tasks for generating information. It is neither practical nor desirable to review every element of behaviour and process in each task, not only because of the time that would require, but also because of the distraction from the programme's objectives. The relevant issues would almost certainly be lost in the welter of information provided. What is needed is a way of directing or focusing the review on the relevant issues, whilst at the same time allowing the participants the opportunity, if needed, to raise any other issues that might have unexpectedly surfaced. If you compare the review process to holding up a mirror for the participants to look at themselves, then the design of the review is a way of directing the mirror to specific areas relevant to the programme's objectives.

Analysis of a task review

A task review can generally be split into three parts:

The initial part of the review is usually designed to get an accurate picture or impression of the group's view of how they have been operating: what processes used, individuals' behaviour, and how successful they have been in the task. Good design will mean that this initial process requires little or no intervention from the trainer. Questions are set up so that they automatically flow around the group without constant prodding or intervention. The intention is to develop a clear picture of how the group saw the task, uninfluenced by any preconceptions from the trainer. It is important that the group develop and 'own' this picture, since it will form the basis for the rest of the review. Because of this it is preferable, if the trainer needs to make any interventions about issues ignored or missed by the group, that he do it at this stage so they become part of the picture.

Whilst it is imperative that the trainer does not influence or contaminate the actual information that the participants produce, the questions and methods that are used to produce this information are almost inevitably going to focus the participants' attention on specific areas. This of course is desirable and is a vital part of the review design; it is the means whereby the trainer is able to ensure that information relevant to the programme objectives is produced and is available for discussion.

The end result of this first section of the review should be an accepted basis (consisting of a number of probably differing perceptions), which can be used in the next section for discussion of changes to process and behaviour for future tasks and back in the workplace.

The second part of the review is usually aimed at identifying ways for individuals and the group to operate more effectively in the next task or project. It often involves putting behaviours and processes into a wider context or framework, using previous experience and/or theories and models. The use of these helps to identify the options for change to the group, who can then start to make choices about more effective behaviours and processes, and how they are going to implement them.

One situation, which occasionally arises on programmes for graduates and supervisors, illustrates this clearly. Having carried out several tasks, the participants have become quite efficient at completing them successfully, planning, managing time and resources, and delegating according to skills. However, whilst the tasks are getting done there is no attention being paid to individuals' needs, and as a result there is a lack of real satisfaction with the results, and the style and atmosphere is often very authoritarian. Introducing the Action Centred Leadership model (see pages 166–7), which is concerned with the idea of managing both the task needs and those of teams and individuals, not only nicely illustrates the problem, it also offers suggestions to deal with it.

The final part of the review is aimed at setting objectives for the next task, so that any changes of behaviour and process that have been decided on are implemented. It is often sufficient to record the changes on a piece of flipchart paper and place it somewhere prominent. If this is not considered sufficient then something more overt may be needed: appointing a member of the group to monitor the changes, setting individual objectives and monitoring them, taking time-outs during the task to bring the group back on target. All these options are effective, and there are many more.

The other important process going on throughout the review is the making of connections back to the workplace. Comparing behaviours, processes and problems as they arise, the question is often: 'Is that how it happens at work?' or 'Does that ever happen at work too?' By asking the questions and making the connections, the trainer is giving the participants an opportunity to pause and think about the current situation at work, perhaps with some new insights or a new perspective, and, where relevant, to start thinking about how it could be changed.

From the above it would seem that the two key areas in the design process are gathering information from the participants, and then interpreting and utilising it.

Most of the issues involved in gathering the information have already been discussed in the section on the 'emotional safety net', in chapter 4, along with suggestions as to how to deal with them. To briefly recap, they are:

- ensuring everyone has an opportunity to express their view
- ensuring that no one individual 'hogs the limelight', and/or hijacks the process in some other way (game playing)
- avoiding potential confusion or conflict related to unspecific language or different perceptions of the same situation.

Solutions to the above are inherent in the use of the review or communication guidelines suggested in that section, along with the idea of specifying within requests and questions the sequence or system for answering them. For example:

> I would like each member of the group in turn to tell the rest of us what was the most stressful part of the task for them, and what made it so. If you could start, John, then we'll carry on round, and after everyone's had their say we'll throw the floor open for further discussion.

There are, however, two further key areas, not yet discussed, which are also highly relevant to the information-gathering process. The first is how to ensure that the information presented by the participants is accurate and uninfluenced by either the views of other members of the group or the trainer's unconscious prejudgements. The techniques used will vary from trainer to trainer depending on their backgrounds, and it is beyond the scope of this book to comment on their validity or effectiveness. What I will do, in the examples given at the end of this chapter, is to describe some of the techniques I have found to be effective and use regularly on programmes.

My personal preference is for techniques that rely on exploring individuals' emotions or feelings during the task, then using these as a way of generating a picture of each individual's perception of how the group functioned. From this basis the review can then move into the subsequent process of putting these individual perceptions into an overall context or framework from which conclusions can be made, and adaptations for future tasks generated.

I prefer this approach, because by focusing on the emotional element for each individual you effectively short-circuit the logical, intellectual, and belief filters that are often imposed in training situations, and which potentially can distort or even confuse people's recollections of events. Instead it enables you to focus directly on what the actual experience was for that individual, and hence have a sound basis on which to build real and relevant outcomes. Related to this are the mnemonic properties of emotion, which can also be used in this phase of the review.

The second key area in the design process is that of putting the information gathered into a context, or framework, which can be used to interpret and utilise it. Here the word 'context' refers to previous experience, either of the participants or the trainer, and the word 'framework' refers to a model or theory. Both can be equally effective.

One of the most effective ways to use context is to tell a well-constructed story in which the relevant experience plays a significant part.

As for frameworks, however, currently there seems to be a complete industry devoted to designing and marketing theories and models, which daily grow in number, diversity and complexity; and any attempt to describe them all fully would be beyond my competence. Listed in the appendix at the end of the book are some of the most commonly used. These have all generated books specific to themselves, so I have only briefly described the areas they cover, and included with each a short hand-out of the type I would give to a group when using them in a review.

Examples of review designs

The remainder of this chapter describes some of the specific and general designs that are regularly used on programmes. Just like the example tasks, they are only a representative half-dozen of the wide range available, and their real function is to illustrate the processes already described, and provide a basis from which you can generate and design your own reviews.

I think it is important to emphasise the need for flexibility in the approach to each review. Having put in the effort and thought needed to design a review for a task, one which will really bring out and focus attention on the salient issues, a trainer can easily become blinkered and miss the fact that the task may have generated a different set of issues entirely, for which the intended review is not at all suitable. This is a common mistake, often made when people first start to review outdoor (and indoor) tasks. However, with an open-minded approach and close observation of the group, it should be easy to avoid. In fact, the examples given below rarely happen exactly as described, as sometimes they are combined, or often models are introduced unexpectedly, because they illustrate a situation particularly well; and groups of course often suggest modifications to them, to suit their own style of operating.

Another option for the trainer is to combine or stack designs, for example using a *Hook* type design (see pages 102–4) to bring a particular issue to the surface, and then as part of the review using the *Six Hats* design (see pages 104–7) to explore that particular issue further.

Finally, a paradoxical element of review design becomes apparent when looking at these designs. In order for the group concerned to be able to discuss the outcomes of the task, and from there to generate their own learning points, they need to generate accurate and clear information as to what those outcomes were, not only for the group as a whole but for each individual. A large part of the trainer's role is ensuring this happens, and in order to do this he or she must on occasion be quite directive. This can usually be avoided later in a programme as the group start to understand the process more clearly; however, until this starts to happen the trainer has no option. To avoid the apparent clash between this behaviour and the trainer's role outlined earlier, the trainer needs to justify any directive behaviour, and ensure that the group understand the reasons for it. Typical examples of this are described in the designs I have labelled the *Hook* and *Six Hats* (see pages 102–7).

Works well – needs improving

This is perhaps the most basic and widely focused review design. It poses the question to the group: 'Which processes, behaviours and outcomes worked well for the group in carrying out the task, and which need to be improved or changed?' There are a number of different ways of phrasing this question, which may be used partly to avoid repetition from review to review, or occasionally to avoid phrasing that might be viewed as threatening by the group. For example, one of the more useful variations is 'PMI' where the participants are asked to put their processes, behaviours and outcomes into three categories: pluses (positives), minuses (negatives), and interesting. With an inquisitive group this can often generate a great deal of useful information and speculation. However the question is phrased, the rest of the process follows a common pattern.

The first section of the review consists of a session in which the participants split into smaller groups, of three or four, and are asked to discuss and then list those processes they feel worked well and those that needed improving. Each group in turn then presents their list to the others, giving them the chance to ask questions.

The trainer summarises and draws all the points together, to present an overall picture. This is then used as the basis for a facilitated discussion on what is needed to improve the main group's effectiveness.

In the early stages of a programme, or when it is used without a personal feedback session, this design focuses almost exclusively on group processes, and is unlikely to produce any but the most basic information about individuals' behaviour. But then in most programmes that is not a problem, since the participants need an initial settling-down or acclimitisation period, experiencing and getting comfortable with the concepts and ideas that underlie the programme, before they get involved in giving and receiving personal feedback.

The final section of the review will consist of 'firming up' the learning points from discussion into specific objectives for the next task, and if they have not already done so, discussing and highlighting any relationships between the issues and solutions generated by the review and similar situations in the workplace.

This is a very basic and broad focus design, and some of the following designs build on these foundations to produce more specific and focused results. Having said that, it is an effective design and is very useful as a way of introducing a group to the processes involved in review.

Against criteria

This is a more focused version of the previous design. Exactly the same processes and format can be used, but the categorisation of experience is different. Here, instead of using the questions above, the group are asked to generate their own criteria against which to review their performance. This can be done in a number of ways. For instance, the most appropriate criteria are often the learning points from previous reviews, especially if the group is not implementing them effectively. Another effective way is to run a session prior to a task, which focuses on a specific area.

The group might be asked to define the key elements in operating effectively as a team, and to prioritise them. These can then be revisited in the first part of the review, with individuals or small groups asked to rate and comment on the team's performance in each of the elements. This can then be used as the basis for the second section of the review.

Another common method is to use preset questions or criteria, listed on a hand-out, with each individual filling in a questionnaire (again assessing the team's performance) and commenting appropriately. The results are then discussed in the group, and again form the basis for the second part of the process. This can be a very effective but unfortunately rather seductive form of review design. In programmes that are skills focused, and do not involve real teams, they can be used occasionally. If used too often they tend to become monotonous and start to stifle the participative and enquiring atmosphere which is an essential part of helping to motivate the participants to explore and learn. My experience, of using them with real teams with real issues, is that they are *not* effective, not only for the reasons given, but because many of the issues generated are unique to the particular team, and the forms merely provide another barrier which has to be overcome in order to bring these issues to the surface and deal with them.

Unfortunately, the appeal of such formatted reviews, with their elements of standardisation, categorisation, and predictability, can be very attractive to an overworked or hard-pressed trainer, and these can feature as a benefit when selling or justifying such a programme. The reality of course is that it is not possible to be sure exactly how a group will react to a specific task, and the regular use of such formatted reviews tends to lull trainers into a routine or rote approach to programmes that is distinctly inappropriate. I well remember reviewing a task on an open programme for human resource consultants some years ago, and being told repeatedly and vehemently by one participant that the review could not possibly be valid unless its basis was a matrix in which criteria could be assessed and measured on a suitable scale. Eventually he allowed me to demonstrate otherwise, but his initial attitude was typical of the approach brought on by reliance on formatted reviews.

Otherwise, however, it is possible to be quite creative with this sort of review, both in generating the criteria, and especially when presenting measurements against them. I have successfully used graphs, pictures and role-plays to do this in an enjoyable and non-threatening manner.

'Model' reviews

This is where a theoretical model or tool is used as the basis for review. It is usually done as a way of introducing it to the participants, so that they can take it away and apply it in specific review and work situations. Normally a model would not be introduced until the second part of a review, and then only if it illustrated the group's experience, or was useful to them in resolving a problem or issue.

Here, however, the model is used to structure the information as it is collected, so that the second stage of the review becomes focused on discussing the relevance and validity of the model; only then is the information processed (within the framework of the model), and use made of it.

Providing the particular tool or model is appropriate for dealing with the outcomes of the task, and the issues generated for the group, this is a very effective way of introducing such ideas. The review design will depend very much on the model or tool; the *Six Hats* review is an example of such a design, focusing on a tool devised by De Bono, which allows the group to examine their own attitudes and how these can affect performance and behaviour.

The other possibility is to use one model as the basis for all the reviews; this may be relevant where the outdoor programme is an intervention, forming part of a larger programme focusing on a particular area. I have also seen stand-alone programmes based entirely on a particular model.

An effective example of this was a team effectiveness programme that I helped design, based on the model presented in one of the *One Minute Manager* books (see the Appendix for details). The tasks were designed to give the group opportunities to move through the various stages of team development, which in this case were labelled: Orientation, Dissatisfaction, Resolution, Production (reasonably analogous to the forming, storming, norming, performing stages described in the Appendix). The reviews were designed to raise participants' awareness of the process, to facilitate their movement through the stages, and to ensure that the results were transferable and relevant to the workplace. Quite deliberately the model was not introduced to the participants until the later stages of the programme, so that it became a framework which they could use to structure their experiences, rather than a filter to distort and perhaps confuse them.

The *Hook*

This design of review is for me one of the most elegant and effective I have come across. When I first started working on commercial programmes I spent a lot of time watching other trainers, watching their techniques, and trying to work out what made them effective. (Many of the trainers themselves were not always able to explain how or why they worked.) The technique I eventually labelled the *Hook*, and which forms the key to this review design, often came up and was always very successful.

The success emanates from two things: the technique very effectively generates individual perceptions of how the task went, and it also focuses directly on the strongest issue generated by the task, whatever it might be.

The first part of the review is of course the process of gathering information. After the task is completed the participants are asked not to discuss it until the review has started, and are taken directly to the review room.

The initial part of the review starts with the trainer asking the group individually to think of a word or phrase that can be used to summarise or represent how they experienced the task. The wording of this request is critical, and should include reference to the following:

- each person is to do this for him- or herself, and not in conjunction with other members of the group
- when they think about their 'experience' of the task, they should remember what they saw happening around them, the voices and sounds they heard, what it felt like physically to do the task, and what their feelings were during the task
- when they all have a word or phrase, the trainer will write them up on the flipchart, and when these are all up, then there will be a chance to find out the meanings behind the words.

It is important that throughout this process discussion and comment is minimised until it is completed.

What has been achieved by this rather structured approach is a word or phrase for each individual that is very strongly 'anchored' to their experience of the task, so that now, when an individual looks at his or her own word or phrase, it will generate the full intensity of experience and emotion created by the task – exactly what is needed to run an effective review.

The next stage is to get each individual to tell the rest of the group what their word or phrase was ('triggering the anchor'), and to describe what it represents. Again it is useful if the trainer prevents discussion of the different views expressed by each individual until everyone has spoken. This completes the information-gathering section of the review.

The next element of the review is to do with processing this information to provide useful learning and adaptations for individuals and the group. I normally use this type of review when I feel that a task may generate frustration or negativity among some of the group, of which others may not be aware. This is often the case in tasks focusing on communication skills or dealing with changing deadlines and objectives. So an effective and simple way to process the information is to remind the group of the consequences in the task that they suffered from, because of frustration and negativity, and then to ask them to suggest ways that these can be avoided in similar situations in the future. These suggestions can then be listed and used as a basis for further discussion about connections and implications in the workplace. This is a particularly effective design to use in conjunction with *In the Kingdom* . . . (see pages 74–7).

It is a very flexible format, and can be used with a wide variety of groups in different situations. I have used it with special needs groups, getting them to draw pictures instead of using words, and I frequently use it at the beginning of a programme as a way of bringing to the surface any hidden agenda. (The technique for this is described later, in the example programme.) The label of *Hooks* has stuck since it seemed to me, at the time, that the word was a hook on which the experience was imbedded and every time you tugged the hook the experience was recreated. Later I read some books on NLP (Neuro-linguistic Programming) and acquired some models for the process, which in that particular jargon is an example of anchoring resource states.

Six Hats

This review is based on a framework for structuring one's thinking suggested by De Bono in his book *Six Thinking Hats* (Penguin, 1990). The basic idea is deceptively simple. There are a number of different attitudes we can adopt when considering an issue; if we wish to have a complete picture of an issue, or think about it in a balanced manner, we must be aware of these attitudes and able to use them to structure our thinking.

This idea is normally used as part of review design for one of two reasons: the concept itself is likely to be useful to the group in the future, either as part of future reviews, or in the workplace; or the group have a marked attitudinal bias (usually, but not always, negative or positive) in the way they look at themselves and their performance, which the trainer feels it would be useful to highlight.

To facilitate this process of awareness of attitude, De Bono categorised and labelled them, linking each with a colour and a metaphorical hat. The idea is that, just like a hat, you 'wear' the appropriate attitude for the task, and change it as needed to fit different circumstances. So if you have been wearing a 'white hat' for a while, or if the situation changes, it might well be sensible to put on your 'green hat' and look at the issue with a different perspective, or from a different angle. The idea of changing hats is important because it reinforces the concept of each individual being able to choose the attitude they wish to take, and their ability to change it if such an attitude is inappropriate.

These coloured hats are used to define six attitudes.

White hat is neutral and objective, is concerned with facts, figures, data, and their consequences.

Red hat is concerned with emotion, and with emotional reactions to a situation.

Green hat looks at creativity and the potential opportunities inherent in a situation. It represents new ideas and growth.

Yellow hat is the optimist's hat, and looks exclusively at the positive aspects of a situation.

Black hat is the pessimist, solely concerned with the negative or potentially negative aspects of a situation.

Blue hat represents an overview of the situation, putting it into a wider context. Also it is the hat used when deciding how to structure your thinking about a situation.

This concept is best used with teams, and a review would be structured as follows:

Before the review starts the trainer needs to prepare six sheets of flipchart paper, ideally each marked with a coloured hat, and pinned up so that the trainer can write on them, and the group can see them all.

After the task has been completed, the participants are brought back into the review room and asked to take a few minutes to reflect individually on the task; and after a suitable pause the trainer asks them to summarise their thoughts and reactions, whatever they were, and to list them as three or four points, again working individually. The key to this initial part of the process is setting up the situation so that each individual produces his or her own, uninfluenced list (as in the previous example), and ensuring the wording of the trainer's request does not presuppose a specific attitude or approach.

The next stage is for the trainer to ask for these points and list them up on the flipcharts; as each point is given it is listed on the sheet with the appropriate hat – but without any explanation of each hat's significance – until all the points have been listed.

At this stage it is likely that, in a reasonably sized team (seven or eight), there will be about 30 points listed, including repetitions.* However, it is extremely unlikely that they will be spread evenly amongst the hats. If the team follows the trainer's expectations, the majority of the points will be under one hat, with the others scattered more generally. Typically, in a team of six fairly negatively biased individuals, 15 of the points will be black hat, five or six will be white, and the rest scattered amongst blue, red and yellow. It is unlikely that there will be any green points, since this sort of negativity seems to exclude creativity as an option.

By this stage I would hope that the team are curious about what the flipcharts represent, and maybe have started to draw their own conclusions. The explanation needs to be delayed until all the points are listed, and the 'shape' or bias of the team's thinking has become apparent. Once this is done the trainer can then explain the concept and how it has been used to look at the way the team view themselves and their performance.

---

* Listing repetitions is always useful as it emphasises the importance of a particular point.

The remainder of the review could focus on two areas:

- the implications to the team of their particular bias in the way they view themselves
- the issues raised by the points themselves.

As in every other review these need to be discussed, put into a framework or into context, suitable adaptations need to be agreed and made, and their relevance and implications in terms of the workplace assessed. This can be done on the flipcharts, with the eventual idea of producing a more balanced view, so for example learning points might go on the green chart, others on the white, and so on.

The *Spider*

This is a more active design, getting the participants up and moving.

Before the start of the review the trainer needs to decide on three or four questions that will highlight the key issues relevant to the group and the task outcomes.

Typically these might be:

- How involved were you in the planning of the task?
- How did your commitment vary during the task?
- What helped you personally to carry out your role in the task?
- What hindered you personally in carrying out your role in the task?

(Obviously, the focus and the level of the questions will vary according to the relevant issues, and the capabilities of the group.)

Each question is then written inside a rough circle drawn in the centre of a piece of flipchart paper, and the pieces of paper are scattered around the room, pinned to the walls, scattered on the floor, and so on. The group members are then given a pen and asked to move around the room and write their answers to the questions on the relevant piece of paper, in the manner shown below, so that the end result is a number of 'spider' diagrams, in which the legs all consist of answers to the questions.

This information can then be developed in a number of ways. One alternative is to summarise it conventionally, put it into

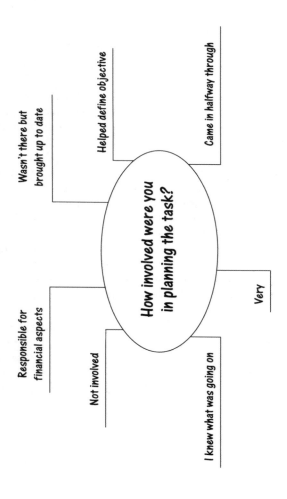

context and use it to generate learning points for the next task and the workplace.

A more adventurous alternative can be very effective with the right group. It is unlikely that all the questions will have generated equally useful amounts of information; one or two of them will have highlighted issues that are much more real and pertinent than the others. The trainer quickly summarises and deals with the others, before focusing on the one (or maybe two) with the most pertinent issues, and developing it/them.

This is done by 'mapping' the issue, taking each answer in turn and asking the individual concerned about its implications and consequences, writing them on the chart, and then in turn looking at these and their implications and consequences, and so on. Whether you choose to follow each answer to its conclusion, or go around the group expanding each answer a 'level' at a time, will depend on your perception of the group. An example of this sort of development of an answer is given on page 110.

At some point if this is a real issue, the answers being generated will start to be relevant to the workplace as well as to the task, and the relevant answers can be physically highlighted on the chart.

This is a very visual technique. You will probably end up with a diagram covering two or three sheets of flipchart paper, and in creating it you have the opportunity to use lots of colours, arrows linking related issues, highlighted areas and so on. (For more ideas on this subject look at *Use Your Head*, published by BBC Books in 1989, or one of Tony Buzan's other books for a description of the process he calls mind mapping.)

The final stage of the review is likely to be very clear cut; a full picture will have been generated of the issue, so generating ways of dealing with it is likely to be a comparatively simple task.

The feelings chart

One of the problems mentioned in passing earlier was dealing with the amount of information generated by the type of tasks I have labelled projects, as these are complex, involve a wide range of skills and issues, and last for several hours. They are used because they provide a much more realistic simulation of the workplace, and hence are ideal for trying out newly acquired

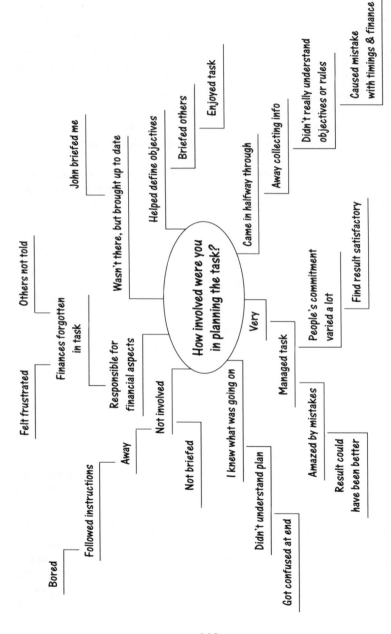

behaviours and skills in an environment which does not necessarily support or immediately reward their use. The issue is twofold: how to filter the information generated by such a project, and isolate and then focus on the issues that are relevant; alternatively, how to ensure that information relevant to these issues is not lost amidst the rest. The design described here is one solution to this problem which can be used either by itself, or in conjunction with other designs.

The basis of the review is a chart or graph similar to the one shown (partly filled in) below, which the trainer needs to have ready at the start of the review.

The review may well start with the trainer explaining the issue outlined above, concerning the need to filter and select amongst

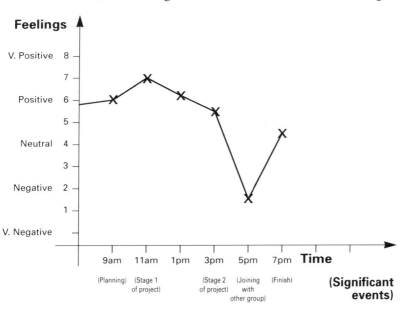

the huge amount of information generated by the project, without losing anything relevant to the issues. He then introduces the idea of using feelings as an indicator, inasmuch as how each individual was feeling at the time is likely to provide a good indication of their perception of how the group was operating, how the task was going, and hence what, if any, the issues were at that point. Alternatively the trainer might decide that, with the particular group in question, it would be more appropriate to fill in the charts straight away, and then talk about it.

The charts are filled in with a time scale along the horizontal axis (suggested by the trainer) and the participants mark points at different times, describing how positive, negative or neutral they were feeling at the time. These points are then joined together to form a curve.

The next stage is particularly important. Each individual is asked to write a couple of words by each high point, low point, period of neutrality, or sudden change in the curve, describing what was going on for them at that time.

These charts form the basis of the remainder of the review. Each member of the group then uses his or her own chart as a basis for presenting his or her experiences in the task. (It is useful if the charts are on A3 paper.) The trainer's job is then to select and highlight the key issues from these mini-presentations and focus the remainder of the review on them.

This type of filtering is common to most types of review, and has an inherent problem, which lies in ensuring that the issues for each individual have been at least recognised, if not discussed and resolved. It is therefore a good idea at the end of any review, especially one of this type, to check and ensure that there are no outstanding issues for any individuals.

Feedback session

Feedback in one form or another is going to be part of almost every outdoor programme. In programmes with objectives focusing mainly on management or leadership skills, there will almost certainly be time devoted to it, either in a separate session, or more likely forming an integral part of the review process, with feedback for the individual leading the task at the end of each review. Briefly described here is a simple group feedback session, which can be run either as part of a review or separately. As described here, it would be most relevant and effective towards the end of a programme.

The session is introduced with a description of what its aims are, and how they are going to be achieved, so that the participants are quite clear about what is going on. The next stage is to remind each participant of the guidelines for giving feedback, and ensure they are conversant and happy with them. Each participant then needs to prepare a piece of flipchart paper with their name at the top and three columns below, headed respectively: 'more of', 'less of', and 'keep the same'.

The trainer then needs to brief the participants on the process for giving feedback. The briefing should make the following points:

- Each person should give feedback to every other member of the group; this is done by writing comments in the appropriate column of that individual's piece of flipchart paper and initialling them.
- The comments should describe specific behaviour that they personally have observed.
- If they find that the comment they wanted to make has already been made, then they should still write it, as the repetition emphasises its importance; but they should also make a serious attempt to add another comment as well.
- They should attempt to write at least one comment in each column, for every individual.

Once everybody has finished writing, each individual can read his or her own sheet, and if necessary ask any questions for clarification. The information generated by this session can then be used by individuals to effect changes in their style of working, and, if relevant, it can be incorporated in the transfer process at the end of the programme.

It is important that the trainer is very clear about the reasons for incorporating the session in a programme, and passes this on to the group. Equally, the process has to be very carefully monitored throughout, to ensure that it remains a useful, positive exercise, and is not allowed to degenerate into a negative and destructive experience for the group and its members.

These then are some examples of different types of review; they vary in their approach, but all address the same problems:

- How to focus on the specific issues relevant to the programme and the group.

- How to gather accurate and uninfluenced information from individuals within the group, relevant to these issues.
- How to use this information to generate relevant, effective learning that can be applied in respect of these issues.
- How to make connections and establish the relevance of this learning to the workplace.
- How to safeguard the welfare of both the individuals and the group in this process.

The designs outlined above work in conjunction with the processes described in the 'emotional safety net' to achieve this effectively, with minimum disruption for the individuals concerned.

7

Transfer

This is undoubtedly one of the more important chapters in this book, because traditionally, along with safety (which has already been discussed), it is one of the two negative issues that are sometimes associated with outdoor programmes. The issue is very simple: how to transfer learning from the programme and implement it in the workplace. An associated issue is the question of how then to measure its effect in the workplace, preferably in financial terms.

The question of measuring effectiveness is dealt with in the next chapter. The remainder of this one focuses on transfer and implementation.

The basis for transfer and implementation

The initial decision to be reached is whether the transfer is to be made by individuals, by the group, or both. Programmes involving culture change or team focused objectives may well warrant a transfer process which involves group transfer. Those involving personal development, or focused on specific skills, would definitely warrant an element of individual transfer, and so on. Trying to define an answer for every eventuality would be excessive; suffice to say that the decision is a commonsense one, dictated by the objectives of the programme and the work circumstances of the participants.

Common to every transfer process is the setting of objectives in one form or another, either by individuals or by teams. The next part of the transfer process involves deciding what these objectives are to be. For a group this is rarely a difficult process, as the walls of the review room will be covered with the outcomes from previous reviews, with those relevant to the workplace highlighted to make them more visible. For individuals these may be relevant, and in addition there are their personal objectives, any feedback they have had on the programme, and observation of the learning and methods of operating of other individuals on the programme. In either case ideas are unlikely to be lacking, so a process of prioritisation will need to take place.

Since the individuals or group are themselves choosing the learning to transfer, and they are choosing them from points which they themselves highlighted as relevant, their initial commitment to this process never becomes an issue. It may of course need support later, but at this stage it can usually be taken as read. If, for some unforeseen reason, it *is* an issue, the atmosphere and relationship between the group and trainer by this time will be such that it will be expressed, and can then be discussed and dealt with.

The final part of this stage in the transfer process is qualifying these ideas, to turn them into workable objectives. The questions I use to achieve this are of course very similar to those used elsewhere in defining objectives for a programme; they are:

Specific. What exactly is going to be changed, done differently, or implemented? In what circumstances, with whom, and when?

Measurable. How will it be apparent that progress is being made, and what will change as a result of moving forward in this area? Can it be quantified or measured?

Achievable. Is the change described above achievable? If this is doubtful, what is likely to get in the way, and what can be done to improve the chances of success?

Relevant. Is the change going to fit in with the overall culture and direction of the organisation? Will it be accepted and recognised?

Time related. When should the measures of success described above be used to review progress?

Support. Where and from whom is support available to achieve this? Where else?

Each of the ideas is subjected to this process so that eventually there are three or four objectives specified in the manner described. It is usually best to limit the objectives to three or four, since more than that are likely to diversify the effort needed to put them into practice, to the extent that it brings their successful implementation into doubt. If there is a strong feeling that more are needed then these can be used in second stage implementation (described later).

The final part of this stage is recording these objectives physically in such a way that they can be referred back to at a later stage.

The next stage in the transfer process is implementing these objectives back in the workplace, and it is at this stage that the whole process is at its most vulnerable. The individual or group is returning from the programme with a set of objectives to be implemented in the workplace, but as yet their manager has at best only a vague idea of what they are likely to be. The people with whom they work will have less of an idea, and individuals who work for the participants are likely to be wary. As we have already discussed in chapter 3, in the section on setting objectives for the programme, a support system is needed to help the participants implement these changes.

There also needs to be a formalised review process, to assess progress against objectives, and if necessary make any adjustments to cater for unexpected problems (or successes). As discussed previously I feel that ideally a two-stage review process is most effective. The first stage provides an opportunity to discuss some of the unexpected problems that have arisen, and to devise solutions to overcome them. I feel that it is important to do this before the memories of the programme, and the commitment and enthusiasm that goes with them, start to fade in the face of resistance and negativity in the workplace. The first review also provides an opportunity, if necessary, to bolster and reinforce that commitment.

The second review would normally take place about eight weeks after the programme, and would focus very much on how successfully the objectives have been implemented, and whether the results of this have matched the participants' expectations. This would then form a significant part of the course evaluation, and effectively marks the end of the process.

Earlier I briefly mentioned 'second-stage implementation'; this phrase refers to another possible outcome from the programme. The process of setting objectives, implementing them, and then reviewing this process, looking at how successful the implementation was, and looking at what problems were encountered, is simply a continuation of the process defined by Kolb and used as the basis for the programme. There is no reason why the process cannot be continued, and used as a forum for continuous development within the workplace. Although it is not a new idea, the use of an outdoor programme which graphically models it is a very elegant and effective way of introducing the concept of continuous development, and the review skills needed to make it work. It is unlikely that most groups of individuals will have the expertise to manage their own review processes straight away, but it is a skill which can be learned, and in the meantime that aspect of the process can be managed for them. This is particularly relevant when working with real teams.

What I have described so far is the basis for an effective system of transfer and implementation; the remainder of this chapter deals with putting it into practice.

Putting it into practice

Normally the last session in the programme is designed to do two things: to review the progress made against the objectives set at the beginning of the programme, and to start the process of transfer. The review of the objectives can be done in a very straightforward and direct manner, and can lead straight into the transfer process, the initial stage of which is usually called action planning.

Fundamental to the process is of course a set of clear, defined objectives, and the first objective of the transfer session is to produce these. As has already been said, defining the areas on which these objectives will focus is unlikely to be a problem, but elaborating them in detail can be a different story. The difficulty often lies in being specific and generating criteria with which to measure progress. If the group are producing individual objectives then they can work in pairs to help each other remedy the problem, with the trainer available as a resource if needed. If producing group objectives the trainer can again facilitate this part of the process.

The second part of the session involves introducing the group to a method of presenting and implementing these objectives in the workplace, and gaining their commitment to it. An important point about this process is that it must be compatible with the company culture and organisation, and therefore there needs to be consultation with the clients before the programme, to ensure that an acceptable or appropriate method is used. Ideally the clients will suggest one for their organisation – after all, implementing change in the workplace is not an unusual situation. This can if necessary be jointly modified by the client and trainer to fit the programme's objectives. Let us now look at some alternatives.

Individual action plans

This is perhaps the most common method of transfer: it simply involves a form which the participant fills in, and which asks a number of questions, intended to take each objective and qualify them in the manner already described. An example is given on page 120. You will notice an additional question is asked: 'How will the individual benefit from implementing the changes?' This is asked in order to give the individual a real personal motive for implementing the change.

Group action plans

These are similar to the individual action plans already described. The same sort of questions are asked of the group, and this is particularly appropriate if working with real teams. It is less vulnerable to lack of support than the individual plan, but when using it in the transfer session it is important to ensure that each member of the group is genuinely committed to the changes listed on it. Reviewing progress with a team is also more demanding than with an individual, which may well be significant if the review process is to be carried out by a manager rather than a trainer.

ACTION PLAN

To be reviewed on _____

I am going to make the following changes in my behaviour.

☐ 1.
☐ 2.
☐ 3.

I am going to do this at the times and places, and with the people below:

The things that will get in my way are:

The people and resources that can help me are:

I will know when I've been successful because the following will happen:

I will benefit from this because:

Both methods are appropriate to most programmes, and especially relevant in those organisations where management by objectives is prevalent. They are also easy formats with which to present outcomes back to the organisation, and especially to management. Most transfer mechanisms will consist solely of one or both of these, and almost all will involve an element of one or the other.

The two examples given below are examples of mechanisms that focus on specific issues; this sort of mechanism requires prior arrangement and discussion with the client organisation, but in terms of results this is usually well worth the effort put in.

Video message

This is a group-orientated method of transfer, often used on culture change programmes where vertical communication is the key issue: typically an 'us and them' situation between management and the workforce. On such a programme one of the key objectives is raising issues before they become major problems. Each group is likely to consist of a vertical slice of the organisation (eg senior manager, junior manager, a couple of foremen, and a shift or team from the shopfloor), and the programme will have concentrated on raising awareness of the complexities and issues that affect different roles within a team, and how they in turn can cause communication problems, with the subsequent problems of lack of trust and even potential hostility.

At the end of the programme the participants are given the resources to make a video highlighting the issues that they feel are current in the workplace. This is done on the understanding that this will be viewed and responded to at board level, preferably by the Managing Director. Obviously this requires serious commitment from the organisation; however, if it is forthcoming, this is a very effective way of quickly short-circuiting barriers to communication, and establishing systems to ensure that they stay down.

Action groups

This is again an organisation-centred method of implementation focusing on cultural change, in this case usually improving horizontal communication between teams. Here the participants who have returned from the programme are from a range of teams, and the programme will have focused on the issues that arise when the teams fail to communicate effectively, and the problems that are subsequently created. At the end of the programme the group will be given a real project to carry out in the workplace, usually a consultancy type role, suggesting and then implementing solutions to real issues. Again, this requires considerable commitment from the organisation in terms of making sufficient time available and in implementing the solutions. This process reinforces the learning from the programme by consolidating the horizontal relationships formed on the programme, and making them useful and significant in the workplace.

Both methods are means of transferring very specific types of learning and take no real account of all the other learning that will have taken place on the programme. Almost invariably they

121

will be used in conjunction with some form of individual action plan to ensure that this learning is not lost.

Two other alternatives are:

Console message

This is a variation on the individual and group action plan, and uses the networked IT consoles which are rapidly becoming a fixture on each individual's desk in many organisations. The system is used as a medium to keep the objectives to the forefront of each individual's mind, flashing reminders at the start of the day, and at other appropriate times, eg before meetings in the diary section, and so on. Competently done, this can be a very effective way of keeping the objectives fresh in an individual's or team's consciousness.

Diaries

This uses similar ideas to those outlined above but focuses on individuals and their diaries. It is very effective with individuals who are dependent on their diaries; for the remainder it is less so, but still worth considering.

The examples given hopefully give some idea of the issues involved, and how they can be dealt with when transferring learning into the organisation. The final part of the process is reviewing progress.

As already mentioned, I favour a two-stage process: the first to maintain enthusiasm and to try to deal with barriers which have arisen in the workplace; the second to look at long-term implementation of the changes, what the results of this have been, and what modifications are still needed.

There are a number of people who may logically be involved in this process apart from the individual or group themselves:

- the trainer who worked with the group or individual on the programme
- the team manager (on a programme involving a real team)
- the team manager's manager

- each individual's manager (on a programme focused on individuals or not involving real teams).

On programmes involving real teams I feel that the first review should be carried out by the team manager, with if appropriate his manager in support. On those more individually focused I feel that it should be carried out by each individual's manager. The reasons behind this are twofold: firstly, it involves them in the process of implementation, and providing the support necessary for this to be a success; secondly, the issues raised in the preliminary review are likely to present practical difficulties in the immediate organisation, which the managers are going to be much more useful and effective in dealing with than the trainer.

However, the second review will raise issues of a different order, which may often involve the manager as well. It thus requires the presence of the trainer, as well as input from the next level up in the organisation. All these people will then be involved in the evaluation of the programme.

Rather than justify this with supposition, it is easier to give a concrete example:

The programme in question was a teambuilding programme, for the management team of a new superstore – about a dozen individuals. The initial review had been handled by the team leader, and had apparently gone very well. The second review happened about nine weeks after the programme, about seven weeks after the store opened. When we arrived, there was a real air of gloom and despondency in the room from the store manager down; even the lady serving the tea looked depressed.

Whilst we were drinking the tea before starting, I took one of the younger managers aside and asked him what was going on, and discovered that one of the things they had decided to do in their action plan was to set and review objectives on a regular basis. One of the objectives they had set involved winning the monthly regional competition that assessed the quality of presentation and service in the stores; and another involved achieving the highest turnover in the region for the same period. When I asked him how they had done, he looked if possible even more depressed and replied: 'We won the competition, but we only came second (out of 48) in the turnover.'

123

To this day I can remember the startled look on his face, when I started laughing and suggested that coming first in the competition, and second out of 48 in the turnover, in their first month of trading, was a creditable performance. The same expression was later repeated on several other faces during the review, and when we left them later that day, they were talking about where to go to celebrate.

This is a classic example of not being able to see the wood for the trees; it is repeated many times in different organisations, and to my mind it illustrates clearly the value of the review being run by someone not directly associated with the participants' workplace.

This then is the transfer process; it is not complicated and in order for it to be successful the requirements are simple:

1. commitment by the participants to real, defined objectives
2. a suitable transfer mechanism (agreed with the client)
3. support from the organisation
4. review.

If this process is going to fall down, in my experience it will happen in one of two places: the trainer failing to facilitate real, defined objectives to which the participants are committed; or (more commonly) lack of real support from the organisation.

In the first case the problem is clearly related either to the trainer's competence, or to the suitability of the programme itself – which again calls the trainer's competence into question.

In the second case the issue is less clear cut, but equally important. Different areas of the organisation may well have different priorities, but if the time, effort, and money spent on a programme is not to be wasted, then it cannot be stressed enough that the potential changes generated in individuals' and groups' behaviour must be supported and encouraged if they are to be successfully implemented.

8

Evaluation

Evaluation is perhaps the most neglected aspect of outdoor programmes, which perhaps explains why it has come to be another unnecessary question mark, detracting from the undoubted validity and effectiveness of the outdoors as a medium for training and development. This neglect seems to me to stem from one of two causes: ignorance both of the ease with which it can be done and its value; and, on occasion, an unwillingness on the part of some clients (condoned by some providers) to stick their necks on the line, and find out exactly what they have achieved.

As a provider of outdoor training, I find this attitude particularly frustrating, because those clients who do carry out an effective programme evaluation are the ones who come back again and again. This is because they recognise the effectiveness of the medium as a tool for change, and so even if their first programme does not fully meet their success criteria, they are prepared to sit down and discuss with the provider how to modify or adjust it to meet the criteria more fully next time. One of the most effective programmes I have come across is the result of six years of collaboration between provider and client. The first programme was reasonably successful and met the client's needs, and as a result of the modifications suggested in the evaluation process, the next was even more successful, and so the process continued. More recently the modifications have been more concerned with meeting the changing needs of the client.

The process described above is one of the values of conducting proper evaluations of an outdoor programme. Another is of course to assess the competence of the provider, the effectiveness of the product and, tied in with this, the cost-effectiveness of the product. If a company is considering running a series of programmes it is worth running a couple of pilots with different providers, and comparing costs with long term results. My own personal experience is that when working with established, reputable providers, the difference in costs (which can sometimes be quite large) is more often a reflection of their respective over-heads, rather than an indication of the potential effectiveness of the programme.

The other major reason for conducting evaluations concerns the whole change process as related to the client organisation. This can be seen as a continuous process which takes the following route: setting in place a number of initiatives (including training programmes) to achieve them; then, after they have been completed, reviewing progress towards those goals, before either defining new goals or modifying the initiatives to make them more successful in achieving the old goals (or doing both simultaneously). Programme evaluation is of course a vital part of this process, and failure to carry it out increases the margins for error. This is also the reason why some organisations are unwilling to carry out evaluations, since these introduce an element of accountability that is not always welcomed.

The evaluation process itself, when properly implemented, consists of two stages.

The first stage is relatively simple and is normally carried out as the very last session of the programme; it usually takes the form of a feedback or evaluation sheet which looks at:

- the participants' immediate reaction to the programme and its content
- feedback on the provider's style and methods
- the administration of the programme
- the domestic arrangements.

The second stage is more complex, and as I have indicated earlier I feel it is usually appropriate to carry it out in conjunction with the second review of the participants' action plans. It is concerned with measuring the long-term effect of the programme in producing change either at an individual level, or if appropriate a team or organisational level. To describe the process involved it is necessary to take a step back and remember the process used to define the client's objectives for the programme.

Part of this involved producing measurable criteria against which progress or success in achieving the objective could be assessed. These criteria not only serve to define and clarify the objectives, but also form the cornerstone of this part of the evaluation. The process of evaluating the programme is simple: once these criteria are defined, they must be measured before the programme, and then (after a suitable interval) measured again after it. Unless other forces have been at work in the intervening period, any changes in the measurements can be considered to be the direct result of the programme itself.

There needs to be a suitable interval after the programme, to ensure that any changes made as a result of the programme have either been properly assimilated into the work patterns of the participants, or have failed in this process and been rejected. As indicated previously, a suitable lapse of time would normally be six weeks or more.

The criteria themselves are of course crucial to the success of this process, and can be split into two types:

Objective: measurable facts, for example staff turnover, sales figures, production, absenteeism and timekeeping, number and length of meetings, the type, origin and quantity of the questions that are asked in them, dissemination and flow of information, and many more.

Subjective: based on opinions and perceptions, and not directly measurable.

Each programme objective would need a number of such criteria from both categories, and with a certain amount of ingenuity it should not prove difficult to devise them to fit any of the potential objectives listed in previous chapters.

This is a short chapter because the foundation of the evaluation process lies in the earlier stage of clarifying and defining the programme's objectives. However, from both the client's and the provider's perspective, it is perhaps the second most important part of the whole structure or system that goes to make up the programme. (The first is safety.)

—————— 9 ——————

Resourcing An Outdoor Programme

The purpose of this chapter is to look at the practicalities and issues involved in resourcing a programme: staffing, venues and equipment. Part of the staffing issues will of course relate to what role you wish to take, and the various considerations that might raise. Another crucial element is assessing and choosing the right outdoor specialists, and finally of course the right venue is often a crucial factor in a programme's success. Let us look at these separately, to see what is involved.

The training staff

The first question to be decided is the level of involvement that you as the client (whether senior manager, line manager, HR or training specialist) wish to have in the programme. It is obviously essential that you are involved in providing the programme's objectives and in defining them as described earlier, and of course in the evaluation process after the programme. It is the area in between that is open to discussion, and there are within it two subjects to discuss:

1. the level of skill that you have in delivering and reviewing such programmes
2. the issues that your participation in the training process might raise for the participants.

Skill breaks down into two areas: knowledge and experience. I hope that this book describes most of the basic knowledge needed, and that where it does not, it describes where to obtain it; so the crucial area is experience.

If you have never experienced an outdoor programme as a participant, it is unlikely that you will have the necessary insight into the processes, from the participants' point of view, to be effective. If you have never run task reviews (as part of an indoor or outdoor programme) for a group of the level involved, or have not spent time observing someone else doing it, then it is not realistic to expect to be able to pick it up as you go along.

As in many other similar professions – coaching, counselling, group therapy, and so on – there are a number of experiences which are necessary before you can function effectively in the role:

- Experience of the area, subject or issues. (In this case working as a manager and part of a team, in a number of environments.)
- Experience of being on the receiving end, so you can empathise with the participants (ie having taken part in an outdoor programme).
- Observing someone else carrying out the role and learning from them.
- Finally carrying out the role yourself and getting detailed feedback from others on the effectiveness of your style and technique.

If you are only part way through this process, there is no reason why it cannot be continued during the programme, and if, as is often the case, we are talking about a series of programmes, then this can be used to move you through these experiences, with a view to reviewing groups in the later programmes of the series.

If the knowledge and experience are already there, then skill is not an issue, and we need to look at the second subject, that of how appropriate it is for a member of the client organisation to work with the group. As a member of that organisation you are more aware of, and involved in, some of the issues and working practices that are current within the organisation; this has several consequences:

- In a review situation you will probably be able to pick up on some issues more quickly than an outsider.
- As an insider you will often be perceived as part of the hierarchy and hence having an axe to grind. This has repercussions when trying to create the open and trusting environment described previously. It can be dealt with, but it is harder for

an insider to do. This issue becomes critical when dealing with certain types of culture change programme (dealing with 'them and us' situations), where there can be a great deal of distrust of, and strong resistance to, the programme's objectives – often reflecting the participants' feelings about management.

- As the client, it is likely that you will have had a considerable input into, and hence understanding of, the programme's objectives, and their implications in the workplace. This is a valuable resource to other trainers on the programme, especially when it comes to the practicalities of transferring learning to the workplace.

- An outsider will be able to draw on experience of a number of different company cultures and bring this to the programme – a very useful attribute.

- When dealing with participants who are peers, or higher in the hierarchy, it is useful to have an outsider fronting the programme (providing they have the necessary credibility).

- Time is often a critical factor. From personal observation few trainers working for companies have the time to design a programme, resource it, and then manage it.

- One of the major benefits of becoming more involved in designing and delivering your own outdoor programmes is cost savings. This is a very difficult area to quantify, because there are so many variables to take into account, but simply by acting as a trainer for one group on a multi-group programme you are likely to be saving £400–700 a day. The more involved you become in the process, and the more responsibility you take for resourcing the programmes, the greater the savings will be. By totally resourcing your own programmes using freelances, it should be possible to save as much as 40 per cent from the cost of contracting the programmes out.

- Self-development: it is a rash person who in the current economic climate does not take every opportunity to develop his or her skills; so if you do not have experience in this field, then to my mind it is almost a criminal waste to pass up the opportunity to learn and develop your own expertise.

These then are some of the issues. The options open to you range from a total do-it-yourself experience to writing the objectives and paying the bill. I would suggest that neither of these is particularly sensible, and some sort of middle ground is appropriate. Certainly on an initial foray into this area it would be rash to jump straight in with both feet. However, assuming the relevant previous experience, a sensible progression might be to work initially with one group in a multi-group programme, with support from another experienced trainer, working with you. When you have built up some experience, then you could operate by yourself with a group, but still in a multi-group programme, thus giving you access to help and support if necessary. The next step would be to design and front a programme, and have an experienced trainer working with another group, so that again, if necessary, support would be available. The final stage of course would be to design and front a programme yourself.

Having decided on your role, the requirements for other training staff should be clarified, and when looking at trainers to work on programmes, there are a number of factors I consider relevant:

Previous experience

In terms of training, I would want to know where they learned review or facilitation skills; ideally this would be with one of the outdoor organisations which have been operating for some time (a minimum of five years, but preferably 10), and have a reputation to match. I would want current experience of operating at the level required for the programme, and a current knowledge of the issues likely to be relevant. In addition I would like to see some evidence of an ongoing programme of self-development, not from any ethical or philosophical point of view, but a pragmatic one, as such evidence provides an indication of flexibility and willingness to learn, both of which the trainer is required to model for the participants.

The background or route into training can sometimes be relevant in terms of contributing special skills to the programme; some have worked as outdoor specialists on programmes, and have over the years built up the skills needed to operate as trainers in this environment, and so are dual skilled. Some come from a commercial management background either direct or via commercial training. Some have backgrounds in counselling or

131

psychology. All can make specific contributions. Having said they can be relevant, however, it is important not to stereotype the attitudes that might go with them.

On a personal level my background before entering this field was as an army officer, and for the first couple of years I found it incredibly frustrating how many people, many of them trainers, took my opinions, attitudes, and areas of knowledge for granted (usually wrongly), without referring to me. I have colleagues who come from counselling or psychology related backgrounds, who are very effective trainers, who suffer from similar problems.

Qualifications

There are very few qualifications directly relevant to the skills needed for this type of work. Most personal development consists of looking at related areas and taking from them concepts, skills and techniques that are relevant. Thus qualifications are unlikely to do more than describe general competence in the field of training.

Personality

This is a simple but important point: the trainer must be able to get on with the group and the other staff. Programmes are intensive and potentially stressful events, often requiring mutual support among the staff; so if there is antagonism or lack of sympathy between trainers then it rapidly becomes apparent to the participants, with the subsequent negative affect on the atmosphere and environment.

The simplest and most effective way of assessing a trainer's suitability is to check his or her experience, and then ask to be put in contact with other organisations with whom he or she has worked recently, on programmes with similar outcomes and similar participants.

Obviously, the actual criteria will vary according to the role of the staff needed, so a trainer to front and direct the programme will need different and more experience than a trainer working with a group as part of a multi-group programme.

There are a number of ways to find such trainers: by recommendation (there are a large number of freelance trainers who work with various training organisations, and asking around will almost certainly turn up some suggestions), by advertising for them, or contracting with an outdoor provider to supply them.

Just to provide a few pointers, however, I list here a few of the 180 companies which currently provide commercial outdoor training. To include them all would take too long and would not be useful. So I have only mentioned those I have direct experience of working with or observing at work, or those which have been long established and have a reputation to match.

ARETÊ – A training consultancy with a considerable history of using outdoor programmes as part of their repertoire.

Aretê Training and Development Ltd
White Cross, South Road
LANCASTER LA1 4XQ   Tel: (0524) 32277

BRATHAY – A long-established provider of outdoor programmes, based in the Lake District.

Brathay Development Training
Brathay Hall, Ambleside
CUMBRIA LA22 0HP   Tel: (05394) 33041

CHALLENGE – A Bristol-based company with substantial experience, and very polished presentation.

Challenge Training Ltd
Great Western Business Park
Churchward Road, Yate
BRISTOL BS17 5NN   Tel: (0454) 315362

DOVE NEST – Another reputable Lake District based company.

Dove Nest Group
Fallbarrow Hall
Bowness on Windermere
CUMBRIA LA23 3DX   Tel: (05394) 45454

EAST – A smaller organisation which nonetheless provides professional and effective programmes.

Executive and Staff Training Ltd
4 Mornington Terrace
Harrogate
N. YORKSHIRE HG1 5DH   Tel: (0423) 531083

IMPACT – One of the better-known companies in the field, with a good reputation and a professional image.

Impact
Cragwood House
Windermere
CUMBRIA LA23 1LQ   Tel: (05394) 88333

LINDLEY TRAINING – Another organisation with a good reputation and substantial experience in the field.

Lindley Training
Swinton Castle, Masham
Nr Ripon
N YORKSHIRE HG4 4JH   Tel: (0765) 689254

MINERVA – A well-established company with a reputation for delivering effective, outcome-orientated programmes.

Minerva Training
Plas Glansevin
Llangadog
DYFED SA19 9AH   Tel: (0550) 777121

NEXT STEP – relatively new to this area, but with a good reputation.

Next Step Management Development Ltd
The Old Stone House, Main Street
Hethe, near Bicester
OXFORDSHIRE OX6 9ES   Tel: (0869) 277098

OUTWARD BOUND TRUST – They have been delivering commercially focused programmes for some time and obviously have a great deal of experience in the use of the outdoors.

The Outward Bound Trust
Chestnut Field, Regents Place
RUGBY CV21 2PJ   Tel: (0788) 560423

WYE ASSOCIATES – Another new company, delivering very upbeat programmes.

Wye Associates
Mewslade House
Blackmore Road
Kelvedon Hatch, Brentwood
ESSEX CM15 0BE   Tel: (0277) 373876

The outdoor staff

The first point to make is that on many programmes it is possible and financially desirable to use staff who can combine training and outdoor expertise. With certain types of group (graduates, supervisors, apprentices and so on) it helps build a positive relationship between the group and trainer. However with groups working at higher levels (middle and senior managers) this is no longer appropriate, as here the trainer needs to focus considerably more on the behaviours and processes within the group, and cannot reasonably be expected to monitor safety as well.

Whether or not the roles are combined does not of course affect the criteria or issues involved in selecting outdoor specialists. At the time of writing (February 1994) there are a number of issues that someone selecting an outdoor specialist needs to be aware of. These are discussed below, before suggesting criteria.

The first issue is the lack of national legislation on minimum standards of safety for any branch of outdoor pursuits, and the lack of even any national Health and Safety guidelines for outdoor training, which is after all a commercial operation, operating as an extension of the workplace, and has been around as such since the early 1950s.

There are a number of national organisations which have in recent years been co-opted into the role of lead bodies for the various outdoor disciplines. Each provides a qualification system that assesses individuals' ability to teach and organise activities safely, and by implication sets minimum safety standards for these disciplines. However, their qualifications are not geared to outdoor training, which requires on occasion additional skills.

Thus the providers have in many cases to decide for themselves what is and is not safe, and as a result many of the larger ones run their own internal assessment and training systems (in conjunction with the national qualifications) to fill in the considerable gaps. In addition, many of the experienced people working in this field obtained their qualifications abroad or in the forces; these qualifications are equally valid but not always tied in to the systems run by the national bodies. Finally, there are still some very experienced people who have been operating for years, but have no formal qualifications whatsoever.

The second issue is to my mind even more serious and a cause for major concern. This is the lack of uniformity in the safety standards applied to different types of client in the outdoor pursuits market. Despite the minimum standards suggested by the lead bodies, it is an observable trend at any climbing and abseiling, canoeing or caving site in the country that different standards of safety are applied to different types of client. The variations are in the experience and expertise of the instructor, instructor/client ratio, level of prior instruction or briefing for the client, condition and age of equipment, level of supervision (obvious or unobtrusive), and result in varying levels of risk to the client.

It should be said that organisations operating with each type of client which fall significantly below minimum standards are usually (but not always) in the minority. I can only attribute the variation to financial concerns or ignorance, although neither of these is acceptable and have in the past (and no doubt will in the future) cost people their lives. A result of this is that for me, when I look for outdoor staff, experience with certain types of client is actually a negative rather than a positive factor.

This is the background against which we operate, and it follows that it is extremely important to exercise care when looking for outdoor staff.

Let us now look at what we want from this person. Of necessity the criteria are somewhat Draconian, but I am working on the better-safe-than-sorry principle:

The first and crucial criterion is considerable current experience of working with adult groups on outdoor training programmes. Initially this must have been with a reputable and well-established provider, who has been operating for at least 10–15 years: in effect working an apprenticeship. This is important because, as mentioned earlier, many of the skills and techniques relevant to instructing this type of group are not covered by any qualifications, and it is likely that only long established companies will have developed a reservoir of appropriate experience and expertise to pass on to their staff. Recent experience must include working with groups of a similar level of seniority to those in the programme. It is absolutely vital that they are asked for references from recent clients and that these are checked thoroughly.

This experience then needs to be related to the type of task to be undertaken in the programme; a programme could involve canoeing, caving, rafting, climbing, abseiling, gorge-descents, mountain walking, construction tasks and many others, each of which requires specialist skills. An instructor is not necessarily competent in all of these areas, so his or her expertise must be checked, and if necessary you must balance the skills among the instructors so that each area necessary to the programme is covered.

Despite my earlier comments about relevance, certain qualifications are a necessary part of the criteria, to demonstrate a minimum competence in the different fields.

First Aid: every instructor should have a specialist first-aid certificate relating to the outdoor environment; it must be current, and renewed on a regular basis.

Mountain walking: any task that involves using heath, moorland, hills or mountains as an environment to set tasks or projects will warrant this sort of qualification. The standard qualification is the Mountain Leadership Certificate (Summer); this is a general qualification, allowing the individual to lead groups in the mountains in summer conditions (ie below the permanent snow line). There are other, more advanced, qualifications, but these are usually unnecessary for the type of activity used on a training programme. The equivalent service qualification, which covers a very similar syllabus, is the Joint Service Mountain Expedition Leader (Summer), and is equally appropriate.

Climbing and abseiling: until recently there was no nationally recognised qualification at the appropriate level. This however has recently been remedied and there is now a Single Pitch Supervisor's Award, sponsored by the British Mountaineering Council and controlled by the Mountain Leader Training Boards. This qualifies individuals to supervise single pitch (ie less than one rope-length high) climbing and abseiling sites. It is newly introduced, but it would be reasonable to expect any competent instructor to possess it by the end of 1994. An appropriate service qualification would be Joint Service Rock Climbing Instructor, which is more than adequate for this level. Until the end of 1994 it may be necessary to check competence in this field by talking to other established and reputable outdoor training organisations with which the instructor has worked.

Canoeing: the British Canoe Union has a well-defined set of qualifications which cover the different variations of canoeing that might be relevant. The minimum level for supervising any canoeing activity is an Instructor's Certificate in the relevant variation – sea, inland, open, kayak, and so on. The service qualifications now closely match the BCU's and confer similar levels of responsibility.

Caving: there is a national caving body, and national caving qualifications; however it is a lot less active than the other bodies and very few people possess these qualifications. So usually competence must again be checked through reference to other reputable outdoor training organisations. The service instructor's qualification is again more than adequate.

Rafting: there is no national qualification in this activity, but to run it competently I would expect a relevant canoeing instructor's certificate, a Bronze Medallion life saving award, and previous experience, as a reasonable indication of competence.

For the remainder of activities normally used on outdoor training programmes there are no formal qualifications available, and expertise in supervising gorge-descents, construction tasks and so on can only be verified through reference to other competent organisations.

Qualifications must always be physically checked by the client, which serves two purposes: recently there have been incidents of people claiming qualifications they do not possess, and also the qualifications themselves usually describe what they cover, to what level and within what limits. Any queries about the qualifications can of course be directed to the lead bodies themselves, which are usually extremely friendly and helpful.

Tied in with the selection of an instructor, or outdoor specialist, is the provision of equipment, and unless you intend to purchase it all new, it will have to be hired or provided as part of an agreement. It is possible to hire boots, caving lamps, helmets, rucksacks and protective clothing, but most other specialist safety equipment, eg ropes, karabiners, caving ladders and so on, cannot and should not be hired from suppliers. Therefore part of the agreement with one of the instructors is likely to involve the provision of specialist safety equipment. There are a number of freelance outdoor specialists, and most offer a complete service including task design, provision of equipment, and other staff if needed.

The provision of equipment also needs to be closely monitored. On most programmes it would be the norm to provide participants with comfortable walking boots, waterproof clothing, and perhaps a fibre-pile top. In addition, the outdoor provider would be expected to provide all the specialist safety equipment required to run the tasks.

This specialist equipment requires specific care and attention.

It is a complex subject and outside the scope of this book to cover in detail; suffice to say that, as a client, you should expect any item of safety equipment that is used in abseiling, caving, climbing, canoeing and similar activities to be checked and where relevant maintained on a regular basis. You would expect this activity to be logged, and in addition you would expect certain items such as climbing and abseil ropes and caving ladders to have individual log books detailing each time they are used; other items such as harnesses, karabiners, and helmets need to be given a finite working-life and to be replaced on a regular, verifiable basis. As far as I am concerned, evidence of these activities, plus qualifications and references as before, serves as the only way to check suitability in this area.

As a final thought, the overriding factor in choosing an outdoor specialist is his or her awareness of and attitude to safety, manifested not in words and assurances, but in observable attention to detail, and awareness of the potential hazards posed by each environment.

The venue

The venue can make or break a programme, as potentially it has a lot to contribute. The building, the style and manner of service, and of course the surroundings, can all combine to help build the atmosphere and add to the impact of the programme. My favourite venues are all set in surroundings which themselves convey a message to the participants as they arrive, that this is not an ordinary programme, and that they can expect to find it interesting, challenging and eventful.

The practicalities which affect the choice of venue are several:

Location

The suitability of any location is determined by two factors. The first is the availability of suitable task sites: there are only certain areas of the country where open country, caves, climbing sites, rivers, etc can be found; and more importantly where access to them is freely available. The second is of course travel time from the workplace to this area.

Time of year

In many areas access to sites is often difficult or slow during the holiday season; this is especially true of the Lakes and the Peak district. Furthermore, in winter there is considerable variation in the climatic conditions, and only some of the areas (South Wales and the South West) can offer acceptable and reasonably reliable weather conditions.

Availability of suitable venues

Choice may be limited by numbers, especially for larger programmes.

Travel time between the sites and the venue

If the task sites are some distance from the venue, a considerable amount of programme time can be wasted. It is often worth considering travelling further afield initially, to a venue close to sites, rather than picking one closer to home which requires a lot of travelling during the programme.

For a London-based company, running a reasonably active programme, suitable areas would be:

the Peak district, except in winter or during the school holidays.

the area around Symonds Yat (just west of Ross-on-Wye), except in the school holidays.

the western and central Brecon Beacons, about an hour further to travel than the other two, but with less associated problems of winter weather and overcrowding.

The venue itself will need to fulfil a number of criteria, aside from the obvious ones of having suitable training facilities:

- Be able to deal with, and be relaxed about, the prospect of a large number of people all returning together possibly wet and dirty, wanting to dry their clothes and boots, and all have a bath at about the same time.

- Be flexible, and be prepared to alter meal times, etc, occasionally to fit your needs, and often at short notice.
- Provide access to grounds in the immediate vicinity, which can be used as sites for short tasks, including construction tasks, which might involve using equipment such as barrels, planks and poles. (Not the gardeners' lovely, manicured lawns!)

The relationship with the venue staff on a programme needs to be close, and carefully monitored, to avoid the sort of potential problems inherent in the above. As a general rule I prefer venues where the standards of catering and accommodation match the expectations of the clients, and the staff are friendly, relaxed, and efficient without being formal. I find this helps to set up a congenial and positive atmosphere, and in addition makes the programme a lot less stressful to run, as problems or requests can be dealt with quickly and easily without them becoming an issue. Ideally it is preferable to have sole use of the venue.

These, then, are the significant areas that need to be addressed when resourcing a programme. In terms of staff, if freelances are being hired, it is imperative that individuals are not taken at face value, and that qualifications and references are checked. If you are a trainer looking to resource your own programme for the first time, with perhaps little experience of outdoor programmes, I strongly suggest that initially you approach and negotiate with one of the established and reputable companies to provide you with the resources, so that in future programmes you have benchmarks of quality and performance against which to assess staff, and tasks.

─────── 10 ───────

Putting It All Together

So far this book has looked at all the separate elements or systems that go to make up an outdoor programme. This is the final chapter, and so it is concerned with putting all these elements together in a programme.

I have chosen a graduate programme, for two groups of six participants, aimed at introducing and developing team management skills, and also with specific objectives aimed at planning and problem-solving skills. The example describes how the various elements are introduced and fitted into the overall structure. I have focused just on the programme itself and not gone into the details of setting the objectives and identifying and measuring success criteria as these are likely to be unique for each organisation.

The programme

Firstly let us look at some likely objectives, skills and issues:

Objectives:	Skills/Issues:
	Communication:
Team management techniques	Listening skills
	Contributing and discussing ideas
Planning skills	Feedback within the group during tasks
	How teams develop
Problem solving	Delegating
	Support and encouragement
	Feedback on individuals' management skills
	Co-ordinating subgroups
	Exploring parameters of tasks
	Dealing with changing goalposts
	Inter-team co-operation vs competition

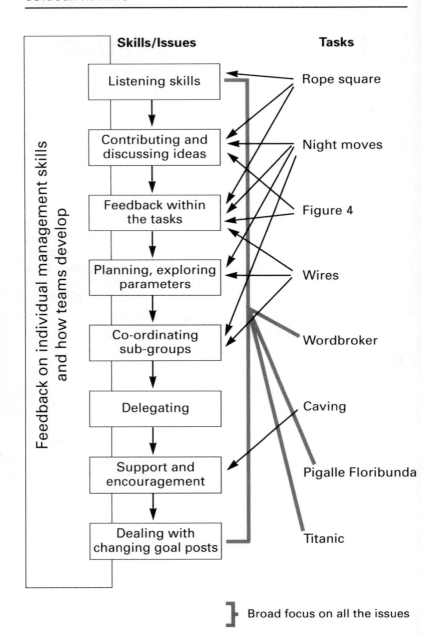

Dealing with the issues in a logical or appropriate order produces a flowchart like the one opposite. This translates into the following timetable:

Day 1

4pm	Arrive at venue, meet staff, allocate rooms, issue any outdoor clothing
5pm	Introduction to programme Icebreaker exercise (*Rope Square*) Introduction to Review Set personal objectives
7pm	Dinner
8.30pm	Exercise (*Night Moves*)
9.45pm	Review

Day 2

9am	Exercise (*Figure 4*)
9.45am	Review
10.30am	Coffee break
10.45am	Exercise (*Wires*)
11.40am	Review
12.30pm	Lunch

1.30pm   Exercise (*Wordbroker*)

4.30pm   Review

5.30pm   Exercise (*Caving*)
Review on site

8pm   Dinner

9.30pm   Indoor session
Review progress on programme and personal
objectives

Day 3

9am   Exercise (*Pigalle Floribunda*)

5pm   Review

7pm   Dinner

Day 4

9am   Exercise (*Titanic*)

11.30am   Review

12.30pm   Lunch

1.30pm   Review objectives and action planning

2.30pm   Course evaluation forms

3pm   Depart.

Normally I would present the other trainer with a package detailing what is likely to be covered in each session, guidelines for the reviews, so that both trainers have a similar baseline from which to operate, and copies of the exercise briefs, with a short explanation of what is involved in them and how they are run. This is perhaps the most effective way to amplify the programme above so I have attached similar material here.

Trainer's notes

Introductory session

This session to be run initially in one group, before splitting into two groups for the remainder of the programme.

1. Points to be covered as one group

- welcome participants to programme
- introduce staff, if appropriate describe backgrounds, and backgrounds of any organisation involved in programme
- admin points: smoking, meal times, availability of bar, where to leave valuables
- safety, role of instructors, fire systems
- collect in health check forms
- introduce programme's objectives, and check they match the participants' expectations; deal with any issues/questions arising
- give out timetables, without exercise titles*
- split into two groups.

2. Points to be covered as two groups

- introduce self in more detail
- explain how programme will work, Kolb cycle
- expand on own and instructor's role, detail the relevant principles that underly the physical safety net, ie they will not be put into a situation that is beyond them (alternative roles available), and must tell the instructor if they feel they are being pressured into such a situation

* These invariably spark off people's preconceptions, and they start to pre-judge their ability to take part in exercises later in the programme; this then becomes an issue affecting all the exercises.

- deal with any hidden agenda, as described below
- introduce first task.

3. Dealing with the hidden agenda

This is a variation on the *Hook* review design, described in Chapter 6.

The participants are asked to think about all the information they have been given, and how they individually feel about being on the programme. They are told also to take into account any other factors that might be affecting them, either at home or at work. They are asked to represent how they feel as a number between one and ten, and jot that number on a piece of paper. One would mean that the only positive thing to be said is that they are actually at the venue; ten would mean extreme enthusiasm.

They are then asked for their numbers, which are written on a flipchart. After acknowledging that obviously each individual has a different system, and hence a nine from one person might be equivalent to a five from another, the trainer then asks the participants individually why they chose the number they did, and what lies behind it. Having listened to each individual he can then pick up on any significant issues raised and either deal with them, or acknowledge and recognise them as appropriate.

Activities, with review guidelines

Rope square

Task

Rope Square is a short communication-skills exercise that is also effective as an ice-breaker. The participants are blindfolded, and then taken to an area where a large rope (40–50 metres) has had its ends tied together and been laid out on the ground, usually in a figure of eight. Each participant is given a piece of rope to hold, and then the brief is read to them.

Brief

This is a verbal brief and should be given to the participants once they all have a grip on the rope:

'Your are all holding a long piece of rope whose ends I have joined together to form a continuous loop.

Your task is to form it into as large and as accurate a square as possible.

There are two rules to the task: you must always keep hold of the rope, and you may not take off your blindfolds.

The task is complete when you all lay the rope on the ground.

You have fifteen minutes to complete it. I will give you time checks after five, ten, and fourteen minutes.

Your time starts now.'

Review

This is really to introduce the participants to the review process, so it should be kept simple.

Before starting the review the communication guidelines need to be introduced. In this case they will be as previously described:

- I use 'I' not -one, we, they, or you.
- I listen without interference: drifting, interrupting or talking aside.
- I take full responsibility for my participation in this pro-gramme.

The review itself is probably best done using something like:

what worked well/what got in the way

After the review the participants need to set personal objectives for the programme. This is perhaps best done in pairs, getting them to ensure that the objectives are specific, measurable, and achievable within the programme.

Finally, introduce them to the idea of feedback for the individuals managing each task, and get them to decide which tasks they want to manage (there are two leadership roles in *Pigalle Floribunda*).

Night moves

Task

The brief for the project (opposite) is fairly self-explanatory, but groups often become so involved in the competitive aspects of the tendering and auctions that they overlook the practicalities of visiting all the points within the time. Very occasionally the groups join together to 'fix' the auction process; this is not an issue since the review can then focus on how this process happened, and how successful overall it was.

POINT VALUES

Point	Value
❏ 1	£700
❏ 2	£700
❏ 3	£650
❏ 4	£500
❏ 5	£600
❏ 6	£500
❏ 7	£450
❏ 8	£450
❏ 9	£500
❏ 10	£800
❏ 11	£850
❏ 12	£1000
❏ 13	£1100
❏ 14	£1200
❏ 15	£1200

Your task is to maximise your capital.

You have a starting budget of £1,000. This may be used to gain more capital as described below.

There are 15 points available to you to visit within walking distance of the hotel.
Visiting a point and correctly answering the question related to the point earns capital.

Visiting all the points in a set gains you a bonus of £1,000. The sets are as follows:

- ❑ Set 1 – Points   1, 7, 9
- ❑ Set 2 – Points   3, 9, 12
- ❑ Set 3 – Points   5, 7, 9

Attached are the points and their values.

The right to visit these points will be auctioned between the two groups. The process will happen in three stages:

- ❑ **Stage 1** – 20 minutes after the start of the task sealed bids must be handed to the auctioneer. Bids will only be accepted for points 1 to 7.

- ❑ **Stage 2** – 15 minutes after the results from Stage 1 have been announced points 8 to 15 will be sold in open auction.

- ❑ **Stage 3** – 15 minutes after the results from Stage 2 have been announced any points not yet disposed of will be available for sale in a Dutch auction.

Once the auction process is complete you will have 30 minutes to collect the points and answer the questions to the auctioneer.

Failure to answer the question correctly within the time, or to visit a point (once having purchased it) will result in the team being penalised the value of the point.

NO HARD LUCK STORIES WILL BE ACCEPTED!

Review

If the group perceive their performance as unsuccessful then a *Hook* type review (see pages 102–4) would work well, focusing on planning skills later in the review. If they perceive themselves as having been successful then a simple format might be helpful. Perhaps working in pairs, they could identify what worked well, and where there was scope for improvement, and then present their findings to the rest of the group.

After this element of the review, introduce guidelines for giving feedback, and initiate feedback for the task manager. Ensure it is recorded on the forms provided and handed to him/her at the end of the session.

Figure 4

Task

As described in the brief (opposite), the task involves passing members of the group through different faces of the structure illustrated below. They are given only a selection of planks and ropes of different lengths.

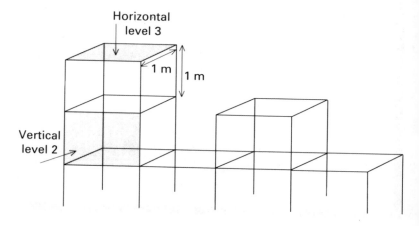

Figure

Your task is to maximise your financial assets.

You have £200 initial capital. Income can be earned by passing members of your team through different faces of the tower. Faces earn as follows:

Vertical level	Horizontal level
1: £30	1: £40
2: £45	2: £50
3: £70	3: £100

Equipment available for use in this exercise can be purchased from the Instructor.

The restrictions on you are:

❑ No-one and nothing may touch the ground inside the restricted area or the structure itself. Anyone who does will be stunned for 5 minutes, returned to their starting point and will have earned no money. Any equipment that touches will be removed from the task permanently.

❑ Only the equipment purchased may be used.

❑ You have 35 minutes to carry out the task.

The Instructor will veto any method of operation he/she considers unsafe.

Review

To be effective in this task the group must not only work well as a team, but plan and co-ordinate well; an effective way to review it is to use a series of questions in the *Spider* type format described on pages 107–9.

Feedback for the manager.

Wires

Task

This is a complex and unusual task. It is set up in a convenient copse, where 'wire' (usually baler twine) is strung in a complex interlinking pattern forming a large number of enclosures of different heights and shapes. In the centre is a large blue barrel to be recovered, and in different parts of the enclosures are a number of pieces of equipment that can be used to aid this process. The brief explains the restrictions that apply.

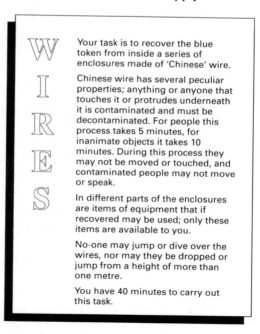

Your task is to recover the blue token from inside a series of enclosures made of 'Chinese' wire.

Chinese wire has several peculiar properties; anything or anyone that touches it or protrudes underneath it is contaminated and must be decontaminated. For people this process takes 5 minutes, for inanimate objects it takes 10 minutes. During this process they may not be moved or touched, and contaminated people may not move or speak.

In different parts of the enclosures are items of equipment that if recovered may be used; only these items are available to you.

No-one may jump or dive over the wires, nor may they be dropped or jump from a height of more than one metre.

You have 40 minutes to carry out this task.

Review

To be successful not only must the group work well together and co-ordinate different individuals, but they must fully explore the parameters of the task, and plan in detail. A good way to review it is to use a design like *Six Hats* (see pages 104–7), although whether or not to use all the colours or go into the model in detail will depend on the group.

Feedback for the manager.

Wordbroker

Task

The brief, though complex (deliberately), is also fairly self-explanatory – see pages 156–60.

Review

This is likely to generate a lot of information, on a broad basis; to filter it and use it constructively I would suggest the following might well be appropriate:

- Ask each individual to put him- or herself in the manager's position and list all the things which he or she felt needed doing or paying attention to in the task, and then list them on a flipchart.
- Ask each individual to repeat the exercise, but from his or her own perspective. Again list them.

Sort the lists into different categories relating to group, task and individual, and use it to introduce the Action Centred Leadership model. This can then be used to provide a framework against which to look at and discuss the outcomes of the task.

*Word*broker

You are one of two advertising agencies with prestigious contracts with the Pan American Trading consortium. To keep the contract you must produce effective poster designs for campaigns advertising two of the three products mentioned below. This must be done within the next 90 minutes. The P.A.T. will purchase the most effective poster design produced for each product; payment will be according to the effectiveness of your poster. The other company are also producing designs for two of these products.

Your task is to maximise your company's financial assets in the next 120 minutes.

The consortium has developed a complex empirical system for measuring the effectiveness of their posters. Each poster must consist of a picture and a caption or a slogan. They allocate numerical values to the semantic content and length of the slogan, and also its position on the poster. This is then totalled and multiplied by a factor of between 1 and 3 depending on their representative's assessment of the originality and/or humour of the design. The higher the end figure, the more effective the design. A more detailed explanation is attached.

The products are:

TATHIN A product that simultaneously gives you a suntan, and induces weight loss – a must for the travel industry.

BUZZ A new electric razor specifically designed for shaving armpits.

SUSHI BURGERS An attempt to make Japanese cuisine more accessible to the European market.

Now to a slightly sensitive subject – of late your company has not been doing well (the exact details are given on the attached sheet), and in order to sell designs you are going to have to get a sample poster printed for each of the products you choose, which is going to be expensive. An outline of printing costs is attached. As you can see, you are going to have to raise more funds.

So, in order to be successful in this task, you will have to co-ordinate and manage three separate but inter-related areas:

❑ Poster design
❑ Fund raising
❑ Finances – balancing running costs and printing and design costs against available funds.

More details are given on the attached sheets.

FUND RAISING

You have the option to purchase a number of tasks which if successfully completed will earn you money. These are divided into three categories which reflect the difficulty and manpower involved in completing them successfully. You may not purchase more than one task every five minutes and there are four available in each category.

Category I

❑ costs £200 to purchase; successful completion earns £400

Category II

❑ costs £300 to purchase; successful completion earns £700

Category III

❑ costs £400 to purchase; successful completion earns £1200.

This category requires a task supervisor. You only have one available to you.

On purchase of a task you will be given a sealed envelope which will contain the details. Category III tasks have time limits, and these start when the envelope is opened.

Current Charges

These break down into three areas:

❑ A basic charge per letter of £10.

❑ Layout and print charges of £400, plus a surcharge of £50 for each minute under 10 minutes given to prepare and print sample posters. No print orders will be accepted after 115 minutes, (eg final design submitted after 110 minutes: no surcharge, after 114 minutes: surcharge £200).

❑ A surcharge per letter depending on position, see diagram below:

Surcharge per letter

	1/3	1/3	1/3
1/3	£5	£10	£5
1/3	£10	£15	£10
1/3	£15	£20	£15

Pan American Trading Consortium

CONFIDENTIAL
MEMO: To all staff, Pan American Trading Consortium

ASSESSMENT SYSTEM, POSTER DESIGNS IN THE EUROPEAN MARKET

This information is confidential and not to be communicated outside the company.

To simplify the system we have produced a board (resembling a giant Scrabble board), which is the current optimum shape for posters in order to maximise consumer appeal. We have given individual letters values, thus giving a numerical value for the appeal of each word. The importance of the position of the caption or slogan is taken into account by the loadings marked on the board. Thus a figure for the effectiveness of a slogan is obtained by multiplying each letter's value by the loading on the board, and then adding together the figures produced to give an overall figure for the slogan or caption.

The overall poster design is then assessed by a company rep., who gives it a loading to represent its Originality/Humour content. This figure will be between 1 and 3 and it is multiplied by the overall figure gained for the slogan to gain an overall total for the poster.

Current policy is that a poster must score at least 1200 on this system before a purchase order can be approved.

Company policy dictates that any advertising agency may only apply for an Originality/Humour loading three times on any one product.

Current rates of pay are £5 per loading point, payable on the 90th minute, after all contract conditions, including sample printing costs, have been met.

FINANCIAL REPORT
Wordbroker Advertising Agency

❏ **Current Assets**: £200.

❏ **Liabilities**: £700 due in 60 minutes, final mortgage payment on premises.

❏ **Credit Limit**: £1,500 – interest rate at previously agreed 40% flat rate; this must be cleared by the 89th minute of the task or you will automatically be made bankrupt, all your assets confiscated and cease trading immediately.

Caving

Task

Caving activity, as described previously (see pages 79–81).

Review

This is more of a coaching situation, where there is a lot of input at the beginning of the task, which rapidly decreases, so that two thirds of the way through it has stopped, and the participants are effectively operating by themselves with just a technical guide. At the end of the task the learning can be reviewed on the spot whilst it is still fresh, and later summarised on a flipchart. The exercise has no formal manager so feedback is not needed.

Indoor session

A short session to introduce and discuss the team development model, and get the team to use it as way of assessing their current state, and what is needed to move forward.

Review the personal and client objectives set, and see if any modifications or changes need to be made, either by the participants or the trainers, in order to meet them.

Pigalle Floribunda

Task

This is a variation on the *Network* project described in chapter 5.

Pigalle Floribunda

Many years ago, before the Champagne region of France had elevated its local product to the deservedly world renowned status of King of Wines, an inferior yet not dissimilar sparkling wine was produced right here in Derbyshire. It was made by fermenting the juice extracted from the roots of the then abundant shrub, *Pigalle floribunda*.

It had been thought, as indeed the opinion of experts confirmed, that the species *Pigalle floribunda* died out a long while ago. However, information has surfaced to suggest that this is not the case.

The recently published memoirs of Professor P. L. Onk have revealed that seeds of the *Pigalle floribunda* have been passed down through many generations of the Professor's family and that in October 1986 one of the seeds was germinated.

Not much is known about the *Pigalle floribunda*, except that it grows 15 centimetres during its first year following germination, and at a rate of 30 centimetres per year thereafter. It reaches its optimum height for wine production during its 4th year. It loses all its leaves during September and its roots are at their best (most swollen), in early to mid October.

The Professor, being a keen fisherman, often stayed at the Hotel. In his will, he decreed that whoever should be staying at the hotel on 31 October 1999 (the date he estimated himself as being the best for harvesting the root crop), should have the opportunity to gather the fruits of his labours. This privilege has fallen on your team.

The Professor, however, was not one for making things easy. The whereabouts of the only surviving *Pigalle floribunda* is recorded inside a locked metal container. The container can be found by working your way through the attached network and by visiting various sites.

The Professor was a clever man and he will expect you to be equally so. If you study the network carefully, as you progress patterns, trends and options will become apparent. If however such things elude you, help is available at sites 25 and 28.

Your team will be working on one side of the network only, and you must establish for yourselves which side that is.

Clues for the other team will be co-located with yours. It is not in the spirit of the exercise to interfere with their clues. Your site clues correspond to the colours on your starter clue envelopes.

To gain access to the metal container you will need to find out the correct number to a four-figure combination lock. The numbers of the combination can be found at sites 14, 15, 17, 22, 23, 30, 32 and 33. The order in which the numbers fall in the combination can be found at sites 13, 16, 18, 21, 26, 27, 31 and 34.

P.T.O.

Sites fall into three categories:

- Those within a 1 km radius of the Hotel.
- Those between a 1 km and 2 km radius of the hotel.
- Those between a 2 km and 4 km radius of the hotel.

You have three methods of travel:

- By foot.
- By bicycle.
- By taxi.

There are two bicycles and one taxi available to you.

Travel by foot is free.

Travel by bicycle costs £20.00 per hour. The minimum charge is £5.00.

Travel by taxi costs £1.00 per mile and £1.00 per minute that the taxi is away from the Hotel. Unfortunately the taxis are driven by W.O.L.I.s (Workers of Limited Intelligence) and must be directed precisely. They are unable to act on their own initiative.

Mileage charges must be paid to the driver every five miles. After every five miles the driver will stop and refuse to go any further unless paid in full. If no payment is forthcoming, he will return to the hotel and no further taxis will be available until the account has been settled.

People may not operate away from the hotel on their own. A minimum of two team members are required for all forms of travel.

If you require it, an instructor will be available to give guidance in the use of bikes. He will also be on hand to give instructions in basic map reading.

When out and about please respect the country code and the laws of the land.

You should aim to reach site 36 by 1700 hours.

GOOD LUCK

Review

This is a large, long project, generating a great deal of information. To filter this I would suggest a 'feelings chart', as described in Chapter 6; thereafter the review will depend on the issues raised. Undoubtedly a major point of discussion will be how the groups interacted, and it may require a plenary session to deal with the issue.

As part of the review it would be useful to introduce the situational leadership model (as described in the Appendix).

Feedback for the two managers.

Titanic

Task

The brief is self-explanatory.

Titanic

Your task is to construct a raft and use it to gain capital using the systems described below.
The project will take place in two stages:

STAGE 1: To design and budget a raft using the equipment indicated to you by the instructor; you have two hours to complete this and at the end of this time a complete budget must be handed to the instructor.
The budget statement must contain the following:

The design criteria being worked to.
Equipment required.
Detailed plans for the raft.

You have a budget of £5,000 to complete the task.

STAGE 2: To load the equipment into a van, travel to a testing site, construct the raft and carry out water tests according to the design criteria below.

DESIGN CRITERIA

1. *Construction time.* Quickness of construction is desirable and will be rewarded as follows:

> Construction within 30 minutes earns £1,200.
> Construction within 40 minutes earns £1,000.
> Construction within 50 minutes earns £600.
> Construction within 60 minutes earns £200.

2. *Carrying capacity.* Each person that the raft can carry during trials earns £200; thus a raft carrying ten people during trials earns £2,000.

3. *Speed.* The raft must be capable of paddling 100 metres within five minutes. Failure to meet this criterion earns a £3,000 fine.

The design criteria being worked to must be stated in the budget; failure to adhere to them during Stage 2 earns a £500 fine per incident.

The raft may not be towed, it must be self-propelled.

Anyone riding on the raft must wear a buoyancy aid and helmet.

During Stage 1 you have a consultancy option. This will cost £500 and will consist of a brief evaluation of the design and likely operational and construction problems.

EQUIPMENT LIST

Plastic Barrel	£500
Metal Barrel	£500
12' Spar	£250
5' Spar	£200
Rope 10mm polypropylene	£250 for 5
Plank 12'	£200
Plank 6'	£150
Scaffold Tubes 3'	£50
4'	£75
6'	£100
8'	£125
Rope 14mm polypropylene	£50
Plank 6'x6"x2"	£100

Review

This is best done by using the implementation of learning points from previous tasks as criteria against which the group can review their performance (also another opportunity to introduce the situational leadership model). This leads neatly into the session after lunch, on action planning.

Reviewing objectives and action planning

The first part of the session involves reviewing progress and learning made in respect of the course and personal objectives.

This then leads into a discussion on how the learning can be implemented in the workplace, what the barriers might be, and how they can be overcome.

Participants are then asked to list (in rough) what changes they would like to make personally in the way they operate in the workplace, and how it would benefit them and the organisation.

The action plans are introduced, and their use is explained fully. Ideally for graduates, they are told that a copy will be given to their line manager, who will review it initially in two weeks, and that it will be reviewed in more detail in six to eight weeks.

Participants are then asked to pair up and use their rough list as a basis to fill in the action plans, using each other as resources to help clarify and specify as required. The trainer also makes him- or herself available as a resource at this point and monitors the process carefully.

The final session of the course is a plenary session in which the participants are each asked to share an outcome of the programme for themselves with the rest of the overall group.

This, then, is an idea of how a complete programme looks. It is a balance between providing a rigid and unresponsive product with a set syllabus, and at the other extreme a lack of overall direction, and inability to measure relevant outcomes.

This is also the end of the book. The intention was to convey an idea of what makes an outdoor programme, how it functions, and how you as an individual can become involved in setting up one for your organisation. I sincerely hope that it has been successful.

Appendix

Some useful Models for review

This Appendix briefly describes a number of models that are often useful in review. The descriptions are brief because most trainers will already be conversant with them and it would take a great deal of space to do them justice, which would in any case be an unnecessary duplication of effort as there are several books devoted to the subject. It is perhaps appropriate, however, to review the manner in which they are used within the system described.

The whole system is founded on a very simple, pragmatic principle: 'Let's look at how we operated, and what the outcomes were, and then let's see what changes we could make to improve these outcomes.' A keystone of this process is gaining a clear and unfiltered picture of how the group operated during the task. Introducing a model beforehand will almost certainly channel the group's thought processes into specific areas, which will in turn affect how the task is carried out and the information presented in the review afterwards. Although this can be a very effective technique, it is not always appropriate.

My own preferred use of models, therefore, is to illustrate situations that have occurred, and then generate options for dealing with similar situations in the future. A group may well identify in review, for example, that the leader's management style was not always appropriate to the circumstances and so created various problems. Introducing the situational leadership model not only illustrates the situation and the problems encountered, but provides a framework within which the leader can make more appropriate choices in the future.

In effect, I am advocating a reactive rather than proactive use of models, which generally ensures that they are relevant, appropriate and useful, and that this is reflected in the programme's outcomes.

Action Centred Leadership

This is a simple, effective, and popular model breaking the leadership or management function into three parts: achieving the task, building the team, and developing individuals. It describes the relationship between the three areas and the consequences of focusing on one to the exclusion of the others. It is particularly effective on programmes aimed at supervisors, graduates, and line managers. It was initially developed by John Adair, and he has described it in a number of books such as *The Skills of Leadership* (Gower, 1984).

The Action Centred Leadership model stresses that, for managers to be effective as leaders, they need to:

a) ensure that the required *tasks* are achieved;
b) ensure that the *needs of the group* for team-work and team spirit are met;
c) ensure that the *needs of each individual* member of the group are met.

The successful leader functions in all three areas and a balance between them is sought.

If the balance is not maintained there may be penalties to pay, for example:

a) If a manager concentrates exclusively on the *task*, by for instance consistently going all out to achieve tasks without paying sufficient attention to training, supporting and motivating the team and individuals, then the short-term goals may be achieved but long-term development of staff will suffer.
b) If the emphasis is all on 'team spirit', a happy work environment may be created but lack of attention toward the *task* will result in *individual* strengths not being developed and under-achievement of the team.

The model is not meant to imply that all areas must be given equal attention at all times. Depending upon the circumstances, it may be appropriate to put extra effort into one area. The primary factor of the model is to remain aware of the importance of all three and to provide a balanced managerial approach.

The way in which these three areas interact is shown in the diagram below.

KEY ACTIONS	TASK	TEAM	INDIVIDUAL
Define objectives	Identify task and constraints	Involve team Share commitment	Clarify objectives Gain acceptance
Plan	Establish priorities Check resources Decide Set standards	Consult Encourage ideas/actions Develop suggestions Structure	Assess skills Set targets Delegate
Brief	Brief the team Check understanding	Answer questions Obtain feedback	Listen Enthuse
Support Monitor	Report progress Maintain standards Discipline	Co-ordinate Reconcile conflict	Advise Assist/Reassure Recognise effort Counsel
Evaluate	Summarise progress Review objectives Replan if necessary	Recognise success Learn from failure	Assess performance Appraise Guide and train

Situational Leadership

This is another simple and effective model focusing on managing and developing individuals. It describes the different styles of leadership appropriate to different stages in the individual's development or competence. It complements the Action Centred model well, and is effective with the same programmes. It is

167

described by Kenneth H. Blanchard, Patricia Zigarmi and Drea Zigarmi in their book, *Leadership and the One-Minute Manager* (Fontana, 1987).

It models the relationship between a leader and a new team member. It can also be helpful when applied to other situational changes such as a team member taking on a new role or learning new skills. Likewise, changes in team membership also affect the competency of other team members and this, too, can affect leader style.

The model assumes that it is desirable for a team member to become competent in his or her role so that the leader may delegate responsibility to him/her. It also states that competence is based on two components: skill level and confidence level.

Directing. A person taking on a new job lacks the skills and/or information that they need to undertake their work. Their confidence is low and so is their skill level. The most effective way to introduce them to their role is a directive style concentrating on task related matters. By doing this they are gaining the skills they need and not being 'dropped in the deep end', only to have a lack of confidence let them down. This can be likened to the ground-based drills undertaken when starting to learn to fly.

Coaching. Once a basic knowledge of the job has been acquired and relevant skills have been learned, the team member will take more initiative to explore his or her role: what is it like to have some responsibility? what are the standards? what if this happens? etc. Flying with dual controls allows for the gradual 'stretching of wings' necessary at this stage. A coaching style of leadership is the most appropriate for the development and application of skills and also helps the member to fit into the team and build a working relationship with the leader.

Supporting. At some point it becomes clear that the individual has sufficient skill to take on the responsibility for his or her job. However, the first time on one's own corresponds to the first solo flight as a pilot – nerve racking! Although no skill development is needed, competence can be undermined by a lack of confidence and so a supporting style is used to help.

Delegating. After a few 'flights' under the different conditions that can normally be expected, competence is gained and the leader can assume a monitoring role, keeping a low profile unless some aspect of the situation changes and a different style is needed.

Preferred Styles. Another aspect of the model is that each person has a preferred style. This applies to the leader, who has a preferred style of leadership, and the team member who has a preferred way of being led.

The Decision Continuum

This is a simple model illustrating the different options for making decisions open to the group, often used when a group is seeking to define roles and responsibilities within itself, or generate options for alternative styles of operating. It was developed by Tannenbaum and Schmidt many years ago.

MAKING DECISIONS

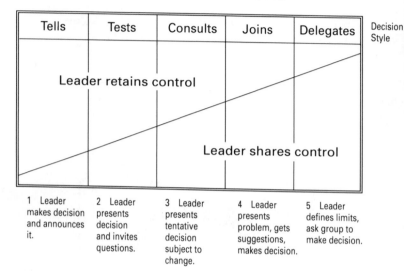

Tells	Tests	Consults	Joins	Delegates	Decision Style

Leader retains control

Leader shares control

| 1 Leader makes decision and announces it. | 2 Leader presents decision and invites questions. | 3 Leader presents tentative decision subject to change. | 4 Leader presents problem, gets suggestions, makes decision. | 5 Leader defines limits, ask group to make decision. |

The Johari Window

This is an increasingly popular model which describes how people are perceived by others and how they perceive themselves. It can be used in a number of ways: certainly when introducing feedback to a potentially resistant group, and also as a model for aspects of self or group development.

	You know	Feedback	You don't know
Others know	Public Area		Blind Area
Others don't know	*Self Disclosure* Hidden Area		Unknown Area

Things known to self and known to others

This could be thought of as the 'transparent' part of your personality. There is free communication between you and others about these aspects of yourself. It is usually the smallest area of Johari's Window.

Things known to self but unknown to others

These are the 'hidden' aspects of your personality. They are things you are aware of in yourself which you choose for various reasons to hide from others. They may include your feelings about others that you keep to yourself.

Things known to others but unknown to self

This could be thought of as your 'blind area'. Others perceive these aspects in you, but you are unaware of them yourself. These aspects can include both strengths and weaknesses you do not realise you have.

Things unknown to self and unknown to others

Both you and others may be unaware of, or perhaps vague about, many aspects of your personality. It is said that you use less than 1 per cent of your brain's potential and thus not much more of your total potential. It may be an unusual set of circumstances that can reveal a previously unknown aspect of your personality, both to yourself and others.

171

The Pyramid and the Pie

These are two short models describing the relative impact of different aspects of communication (from Albert Mehrabian), and how people can communicate on different levels. Useful to illustrate particular situations.

Levels of communication

```
        1
       Peak

        2
     Feelings

        3
  Ideas & Judgements

        4
   Gossip & Facts

        5
  Ritual & Cliché
```

As openness, trust and objectivity increase, the level of communication can move upwards. Each level represents acceptance of greater interpersonal 'risk-taking' between participants.

Communication

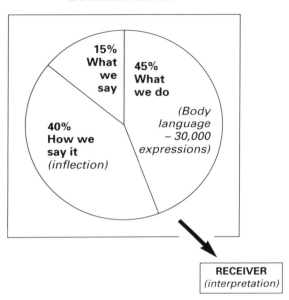

RECEIVER
(interpretation)

Team Development Model

There are a number of these, which are all reasonably similar; the one illustrated here is the simplest. The diagram shows the different stages a team goes through in its development, but it deliberately does not show how they can also regress if circumstances change or management proves ineffective. Another similar and very effective model is described in the book *The One Minute Manager Builds High-Performing Teams* by Kenneth Blanchard, Donald Carew and Eunice Paresi-Carew (Fontana, 1993). Some outdoor providers base entire teambuilding programmes around the models and processes suggested in this book.

Team Development: The Four Stages

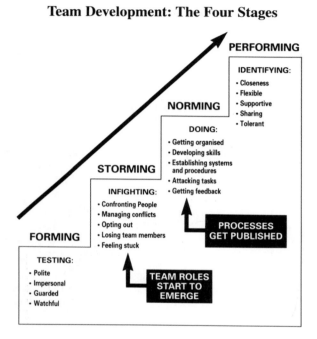

Maslow's Hierarchy of Needs

This is an expression by Maslow of the priority of individuals' needs. At the bottom of the pyramid are the most basic needs, which have to be fulfilled before those higher up the pyramid are addressed. It is particularly useful when talking about motivating individuals. It is described in more detail in *Dominance, Self-Esteem, Self-Actualisation: Germinal Papers of A H Maslow*, edited by Richard J Lowry (Wadsworth Publishing Co., Inc.)

Maslow's Hierarchy of Needs

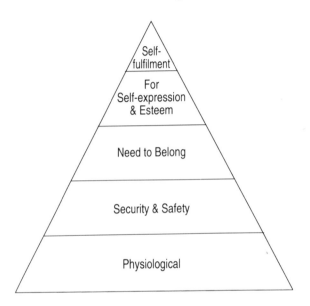

- ● SELF-FULFILMENT
  Inventive/Creative; Self-expression; Mature; Success; Fully stretch capabilities; Achieve high goals; Reach the ideal.

- ● FOR SELF-EXPRESSION & ESTEEM
  To feel confident & useful; Independence; Self-respect & respect of others; Skilful; Reputation; Prestige; Recognition.

- ● NEED TO BELONG
  To be part of a team; Accepted by work unit; Be with others; To have friends; Popular; Affection; Sex; Love & be loved.

- ● SECURITY & SAFETY
  Comfort; Shelter (rented) → (owned); Warmth; Pension; Savings/Wealth; High living standards; Insurance.

- ● PHYSIOLOGICAL
  Water; Air; Food; Rest, sleep; Sex for procreation.

DEVELOPING SKILLS

Other titles in this series

Assessment Centres
Second edition
Charles Woodruffe

This acclaimed book explains how assessment centres can be a crucial tool for selection and development.

Charles Woodruffe examines:

- design and delivery
- personnel and participants
- feedback
- training techniques
- validation techniques

This revised second edition includes far more detailed consideration of development centres, the latest thinking on critical competencies, and likely future issues.

0 85292 545 X

Training Needs
Analysis and Evaluation
Frances and Roland Bee

Roland and Frances Bee argue that training needs must be driven from business needs and a corporate strategy developed in response to external and internal stimuli.

Once the need has been clearly specified, all the more technical issues fall easily into place.

Using many examples, this clear and practical guide describes a systematic four-stage evaluation process which allows managers to assess whether training has been successfully transferred to the workplace, whether it serves organisational objectives and provides value for money.

0 85292 547 6

Everyone Needs a Mentor
How to foster talent within the organisation
Second edition

David Clutterbuck

Mentoring, once predominantly a North American phenomenon, has taken root in the UK and Europe. David Clutterbuck's popular book draws on the practical experience of British and European companies to illustrate best practice. The experience of these companies shows that mentoring is a valuable, rapid and cost-effective method of developing junior managers, recent graduates and minorities.

The book looks at how mentoring works, the benefits to the company, to the mentor and to the protege, and how to avoid some of the problems inherent within the organisation.

'This is a splendid little book for all those who want to know what mentoring is and how the process can help people to develop at work.'
Transition

0 85292 461 5

Job Analysis
A practical guide for managers
Second edition

Michael Pearn and Rajvinder Kandola

Job analysis offers a series of invaluable techniques for assessing how work is done – and how it could be done better.

Whenever managers try to define excellence or draw up job descriptions, identify career paths or evaluate a training scheme, job, task and role analysis count as vital tools. In this well-established text, two leading occupational psychologists examine the most effective modern methods and illustrate their use with fascinating real-life examples. Their extensively revised second edition includes full discussion of recent developments like the Work Profiling System and the competency framework. For all personnel specialists and many other managers, it offers a superb introduction to a crucial (but often neglected) area of expertise.

'This is essentially a practical text that focuses on an area which is of crucial importance to a manager and demonstrates how much more there is to 'job analysis' than time and motion study. It is brief, clear and to the point.'
Modern Management

0 85292 542 5

Top Class Management
Lessons for Effectiveness
Edwin Singer and Richard Graham

Effective training builds on managers' need to acquire – and practise – a wide range of new skills. This superb book provides a compact portfolio of all the essential elements.

Drawing extensively on the authors' highly successful courses for British Rail and a leading rubber company, as well as many incisive examples from retailing, manufacturing, transportation and the public sector, it explains the nature of business, the market economy and management professionalism. Later chapters set out the basic philosophy and principles of:

- learning by doing
- making things happen – through people
- do-it-yourself strategic planning
- listening to the market and caring for customers
- harnessing data and measuring results
- working with groups and leading from the front
- reviewing and improving your performance
- becoming a better manager.

For anyone involved in developing managers or establishing a learning organisation – and all managers keen to get ahead – Graham and Singer offer both plentiful practical guidance and a unique stimulus to success.

0 85292 530 1

Interviews: Skills and strategy
John Courtis

This incisive book shows how a well prepared strategy and the right searching questions can lead to far more effective and quicker interviews. All the vital skills are included:

- attracting better candidates
- filtering out no-hopers
- selling the company
- spotting potential
- techniques for appraisal and counselling interviews
- support from testing and scored bio-data

0 85292 406 2

Using the HR Consultant
Achieving results, adding value
Michael Armstrong

Michael Armstrong, one of Britain's best-known business writers, examines the different skills supplied by HR consultants, how they operate, and the best (and some less good) reasons for using them. He gives advice on:

- setting and communicating objectives
- selecting the right consultant
- building teams and gaining staff commitment
- managing the project for maximum effectiveness
- coping with problems and parting company
- implementing consultants suggestions

0 85292 546 8

Effective Change
Twenty ways to make it happen
Andrew Leigh

Today's managers live in times of turbulent change. They can ignore change, resist it – or use it to improve their organisation.

Andrew Leigh has distilled the wisdom of the experts and created an invaluable toolkit of strategies, procedures and techniques for achieving effective change. His twenty ways include:

- team building
- commitment
- experimenting
- participative decision making
- tracking
- force field analysis
- verbal skills.

0 85292 412 7

Turning People On
The motivation challenge
Andrew Sargent

How does the manager gain the positive commitment of the work-force? What measures are necessary to motivate employees and make them effective members of the organisation?

Andrew Sargent explains the issues, the theories expounded by behavioural scientists, the barriers to motivation, the crucial influence of the personnel expert and, through description of actual case studies, the role of supervisors. He offers positive, practical and informative guidance to achieving harmonisation and motivating the team.

Above all, the book focuses on constructive analysis of the challenge of motivation and practical help in making it happen.

0 85292 444 5

Raising the Profile
Marketing the HR Function
David Clutterbuck and Desmond Dearlove

HR departments *know* they provide a vital service to their internal customers – so why do they often enjoy only grudging **respect?**

Largely, suggest David Clutterbuck and Desmond Dearlove in this stimulating handbook, because they neglect basic *marketing* skills. By segmenting their 'client base', developing the 'key accounts', soliciting and responding to feedback, creating an HR brand and constantly com-municating the key messages, personnel practitioners can soon transform the way they are perceived. A commitment to quality and customer care is no optional extra, but clear evidence of HR professionalism; this invaluable book explains the essential techniques involved.

0 85292 526 3

For further information on the full range of IPM titles
please contact

The Publications Department
The Institute of Personnel Management
IPM House
Camp Road
London SW19 4UX
Tel: (081) 946 9100